"Whoop and Drive 'er!"

Growing Up in Aroostook County, Maine

For Anne,
a good friend & gifted artist.
All the Best,
David 3/1/15

a memoir by

David Estey

"Whoop and Drive 'er"
Growing Up in Aroostook County, Maine

©2014 David Estey

ISBN 13: 978-1-63381-012-9

Designed and produced by
Maine Authors Publishing
558 Main Street, Rockland, Maine 04841
www.maineauthorspublishing.com

Printed in the United States of America

For the Estey and Doughty families and my teachers,
who made me feel loved, secure and confident growing up.

On the cover: *Aroostook*, 1999 oil, 36˝ x 48˝ (on loan to UMaine Hutchinson Center, Belfast)

CONTENTS

INTRODUCTION

The title expression was a popular one when I grew up in "the County," as Aroostook came to be known. The saying is an apt description of the can-do attitude in the often harsh economic and physical environment of northern Maine. I'll explain its origins later in the book.

This book is a collection of stories, characters and experiences I've enjoyed talking about over the years. Family and friends encouraged me to write them down before they are lost.

Most, but not all, of the memories are humorous. Some are just odd or poignant. Some narrative is included to put the stories and me in context. Although a lot of them are about growing up in Aroostook County, Maine, I've also included people, places, and incidents in later life: living on the Maine coast, travel in Europe, time in the army, managing public affairs in the IRS, dealing with the news media, living in the South, and being an artist. In a few cases, I've changed the names, so as not to be embarrassing or hurtful to real people. I hope I've succeeded in that. If I've missed the mark here and there, I sincerely apologize.

I have not attempted to write a complete, historical or even balanced view of the people, places, experiences and relationships of my life, only some remembrances that have stuck with me over the years. Some people have loomed much larger than others in this collection. That is not just a reflection of my affection for them or a lack thereof, but that I spent more time with some or that they offered a greater wealth of humorous memories. My father-in-law, Cecil Emery, is a good example, with his dry wit and Maine sense of humor.

I hope you will enjoy reading these stories as much as I've enjoyed telling them over the years. To help bring them to life, I've inserted related photos or drawings and paintings I happened to do over the years. If you're from the County or are reflected here, I also hope the descriptions ring fair and true.

Please bear with me through the first several pages of family stuff as I set up the context of who I am and where I came from.

James Estey, 1983 charcoal & chalk, 27" x 21"

The Esteys

My paternal grandparents, James Albert and Margaret Rebecca (McNeil) Estey, came to Fort Fairfield, Maine, from Fredericton, New Brunswick, Canada, in 1926. Their firstborn and my father, Vincent Randolph, was five years old.

They had six other children, including two sets of twins, one of whom died very young. My grandfather had been one of those guys who drove logs down the river by jumping from one to the other to break up jams. In his early days at the Fort, as locals say, he broke mustangs for a farm in Stevensville. They had come in by train to the Canadian Pacific Railroad yard and were herded up through town. How he learned to do that, I never heard. As his family grew, he was advised by his boss to take an opening as custodian at the high school, which he did, becoming a well-known and well-liked fixture there. He moved his family to a bigger house at what was then 45 Elm Street and retired there in 1958. A year later, he was dead, I think from no longer having a job to do. Gram died 39 years later at the age of 102.

Grampy never learned to read and write. He was a laborer whose job it was to provide. Gram took care of business. They were church-going Irish Catholics, with Gram making extra money each week by mangling (ironing) towels for Spike Delano's Barber Shop and baking bread and rolls for several families around town. They raised my cousin, Wayne, who was the son of their daughter, Alda. He was two years older than me, so I spent a lot of time there playing with him. When my family moved to Belfast, Maine in 1957, Dad arranged that I stay at my grandparents' house to finish my freshman year, as I was president of the class and into sports, and so on. My math teacher, Aubrey Flanders, rented the bedroom next to mine, and he gave me the *New York Times* every Sunday after he finished with it. I first learned of Vincent Van Gogh by reading a review of the movie *Lust for Life*, with Kirk Douglas. However, not being in Belfast, I missed the filming of *Peyton Place* that year at Crosby High School.

One day, Gramp came home for lunch to find a new kind of bread on the table. "What do you call that there?" he asked. Gram explained it was that new store-bought bread and asked him to try it and see what he thought.

"Here's what I think of it," he said, rolling a slice into a ball and bouncing it across the table.

Another time at lunch, he announced that he had something to tell me but didn't want me to get a big head. "I was talking today to the new principal (Daniel Center)," he said, "and he told me you are a genius and you can be anything you want to be." I don't remember Gramp ever taking much interest before in what I was doing, other than to ask about my drawings, "What do you call that there?"

Many decades later, I learned that the Estey family can be traced back to Beatrice and Isabella d'Este, who was married to the Duke of Milan, Ludovico Sforza, and that both women were drawn and painted by Leonardo da Vinci during the Renaissance. My wife, Karen, and I visited the sumptuous ruins of Villa d'Este outside Rome in 1995.

Margaret Rebecca Estey

Margaret Rebecca

Dad's mother remained mentally sharp right up until her death at 102. She could still beat Dad at cards and often did.

He described one game of canasta when, after trumping him with a good hand, she'd rejoiced in slapping down her cards and rapping those old knuckles on the table. "Geez, Mom, take it easy," he'd said. "I'm your son, you know."

"There are no friends or relatives in cards," was all she said.

A few hands later, she did the same thing. "Mom, give me a break," Dad pleaded.

"Give ya nothin', take ya nowhere," was her response.

I think it was in her 100th year that, as Fort Fairfield's oldest citizen, she was asked to cut the ribbon for the elder care facility that would replace the hospital.

We were there when the organizer pinned a corsage on her, gave her a big pair of wooden scissors, explained that she would just hold them on the ribbon, not actually cut it, and asked whether she could do that. She said she could, and they went ahead with their introductions and speeches. I kept watching her, thinking that she really wanted to cut that ribbon.

Finally, they finished the dedication, took pictures, removed the wooden scissors, and invited everybody to have refreshments. Her youngest son, James "Rollie," later wheeled her out to the car, took her home, and was lifting her into her rocker by the window when she whispered something to him. "What's that, Mom?" he asked.

This frail, little Irish Catholic, a dedicated churchgoer who never condoned cursing and was already a saint in the eyes of the family, repeated, "That was bullshit: I never cut that ribbon."

The Doughtys

My maternal grandparents, William and Janet (Coes) Doughty, raised 18 of their 20 children on a farm built by his grandfather, Samuel Everett, for which their road outside of Fort Fairfield was named. It was often said that there were more Doughtys than people in Fort Fairfield.

I never met my maternal grandmother, as she died in childbirth at age 45, nine years before I was born. Her obituary made clear that she was just plain worn out, but that she had been a loyal, hard-working wife and mother from her marriage at 16. They raised six girls and twelve boys, seven of whom were born before the first girl. They were all hard workers and the family had a good reputation for honesty and fairness. Bill Doughty died of cancer 13 years later, on January 4, 1946, when I was three. It was just nine days after the death of my five-year old brother, Kenny, whom he loved dearly.

I loved going out to the Doughty farm and I spent a lot of time there, especially after Kenny died and I became old enough to be some company for my uncles as they went about their chores. It was about five miles out of town, right on the Canadian border. I

Doughty Family circa 1927, with 16 of 20 children. Front row (l to r): Harry, Ralph, Franklin, Kathleen, Glenda, Arthur, Mildred & Madeline (twins), and Helen. Back Row: Walter, Clarence, Luther, Mother (with Gertrude), Father (with Bruce), Rodolph and Robert.

could climb up in the fields against the boundary line and look back over the town and the Aroostook River. There were many buildings: a barn, stable, machine shed, henhouse, springhouse, woodshed, summer and winter outhouses, and the two-story farmhouse with many gables and a wrap-around porch. There was an apple orchard with honeybees, a little brook fed by a cold, clear spring, and a private road going through the woods to Aunt Helen's place in Canada, approved by the border patrol. What a great place for a kid to grow up, especially as I didn't have to work the farm. I did get to play fairly young at haying, pulling mustard, picking rocks, picking potatoes, stacking wood, and even driving truck and tractor.

Most of my uncles joined the service during World War II, and I was very proud to see them at the front of the Memorial Day parades and such when they returned. They had sent me and my sister Barbara gifts and letters while they were gone. When they came back, they all got married and started families. I have two sisters and a lot of cousins born in 1947 and '49. Meanwhile, they would often pick me up whenever they came to town, so I got to spend a lot of time hanging out with them and going out to the farm before their own kids got big

enough to do those things. I always felt very close to my uncles.

Aunt Madeline Hansen, my mother's twin sister, was the only unmarried woman left on the farm when my grandfather died, so he left it to her and the single boys. He stipulated that she become the guardian of Charles, the youngest, until he came of age, which she did—and long after that. One of the brothers, Ralph, from whom I got my middle name, bought the others out and became owner of the farm.

I'm very proud of my Doughty heritage and grateful for their love and caring.

Vincent
Randolph
Estey

Dad

Vincent Randolph Estey was a very smart man. I always thought he knew everything and could do anything. He considered himself a man's man. In many ways he was, but not in all ways.

He always liked to hang out with the guys—firemen, policemen, and veterans—but he also captured and enjoyed the attention of women. As a young man, he continued to sow wild oats well into his marriage, drinking and carousing with his buddies. He was always well liked, with a quick wit, great sense of humor, and flirtatious manner. He loved sports, made small wagers on games, played the horses, and played golf. Over the years, he spent a lot of time at VFW and American Legion halls, where guy talk flowed freely, along with inexpensive drinks. He held official positions in different veterans' organizations, as well as with police and fire auxiliaries. Yet, there was another side to Dad.

Tough as he often seemed to us kids, as a disciplinarian not to be crossed, we also knew he (and daughter Cheryl) would be the first to tear up during a *Lassie* episode. He was very sentimental and loved dogs, so that was understandable. Whenever something

10

deeply moving came on TV, we would all look over to see Dad wiping a tear. He and Cheryl almost always took the side of the underdog.

Early on, Dad and I both liked sports, and he made half-hearted attempts to teach me baseball. His big failing there was buying me a cheap, flat glove with no pocket, making it impossible for me to catch anything or become enthused about the prospect. I was never quite the sports-minded macho guy that Dad was, and we both knew it, so I got a special kick out of an exchange between us late in his life. I was telling him about an article in the paper saying men whose index and third fingers were the same length had stronger feminine tendencies. While I was reading it to him, I saw, out of the corner of my eye, that he was secretly examining his fingers and finding that to be the case.

Dad then wanted to see my hands, which were clearly not like that. He became very quiet and we had no further discussion about it.

Hands

Long after her divorce from Dad, Mom visited my family in Somerdale, NJ and took my picture as I arrived home from the office in my pinstriped suit and tie. In the photograph, I was standing in front of a fancy clock, and it reminded me of the President in front of his official seal. Something else seemed familiar. My hands folded in front of me looked just like Dad's hands in one of my wedding pictures. I was telling him all of this on the phone later and asked whether he wanted a copy of the picture.

"No," he said, "I'd rather remember you the way you were."

Mildred (imagined composite), 2002 red chalk, 17" X 14"

Mom

Mildred Ruth Estey was a private person, quiet and shy, but she could be a fierce protector of her family and what she thought was rightfully hers. She most valued family and work. After all, she was a Doughty.

Throughout her lifetime, she shared her innermost thoughts with her beloved twin, Madeline, whom Dad had dated first. After we moved to Belfast, Mom and Mad exchanged weekly postcards and letters. When they got together, nothing and nobody was immune from their tongues. They kept track of their siblings, their nieces and nephews and their kids. Mom saved hundreds of family photos and articles. The Doughty family was close knit.

As a housewife and mother, Mom worked hard all her life. In tough times, she did whatever she could to help provide for her family, whether by scrimping and saving or hiring out. It often fell to her to make ends meet and put something on the table. I remember her sitting up nights, after hard days of picking potatoes, sewing zippers on old men's pants, and doing other repairs for the local cleaners. Long after she should have retired, she worked as a cook in the "old ladies home" in Belfast, along with her older sister, Kay, who was the matron.

Min, as her siblings called her, was a simple woman in many ways, but she secretly wanted to see faraway places, like Japan. She rarely got far from Maine, but she was able to travel the world through the miracle of television. One time I found her carefully reading volume after volume of my *World Book Encyclopedia*. She was more interested in relationships between people and their families, whether in real life, romance magazines and soap operas, or among well-known personalities. Her reaction to disruption of her TV soaps by tedious world affairs and all that "culch" was often, "Yes, now I betcha!"

Mom had a full helping of life's joys and sorrows. She survived the accidents and illnesses of her youth. She suffered the loss of her firstborn son, Kenny, when he was five, and some forty years later, the loss of a granddaughter, Barbara's daughter Melissa. Late in life she also survived the loss of her marriage.

She twice beat the effects of stroke, the first one in her forties. By the time of the third, through painful and joyful experiences, her faith in God had become real. Perhaps she was never stronger, or nobler, than when she set about to die with dignity and grace, and steadfastly carried it out.

She left us with a sense of pride in family and place and a sense of goodness and self-reliance.

Kenny

Kenneth Randolph was my parents' firstborn. He died of diphtheria the day after Christmas 1945, when he was five and I was three.

Kenny was the darling of the Doughty family and the apple of Grandfather's eye. He spent a lot of time out on the farm, and he would no sooner get back in town than one of the boys would pick him up to go back out. He had been given a kitten just before Christmas and they were inseparable. On Christmas Day he took ill. Mom and Dad took him to the local hospital and he was admitted overnight. He died suddenly the next morning. The cat died not long after and so did my grandfather. Papa died of cancer on January 4, 1946, but the family felt that he died of a broken heart. They also blamed the cat for Kenny's death.

Kenny was an adventurous and handsome boy with a freckled face. We looked a lot alike but I was still pudgy then and looked more like Spanky from the Little Rascals movies. People told of our raiding the henhouse on the farm and both emerging with a bantam hen in a bag on our shoulders. I don't remember that but I do remember playing with Kenny on a wooden airplane with pedals. When he died, Mom bronzed his baby shoes and put away all of his toys, including the airplane. I then became the child companion of the Doughty brothers.

Pit, Ta, Boob

These were the affectionate nicknames I gave my younger sisters.

Barbara, the oldest, became "Boob" because she had a youthful crush on Georgie Bubar, not because of any physical attributes, as she would readily attest. Cheryl, the middle sister, became "Tahoo," for some unknown reason. Maybe I just liked the exotic-sounding word Tah-hooo. Alana, our youngest sister, was clearly the pet in the family, so she became "Pet" and eventually "Pit."

Aunt Madeline and others in the family gave the girls nicer nicknames, "Bunny," "Deedee," and "Pooty," respectively. If my sisters had a nickname for me, I don't remember or never knew it, except for "Mom's favorite," late in life. I don't know whether that was well deserved or only their excuse mechanism, but I *was* the only boy.

Barbara, Cheryl & Alana at Presque Isle

15

Dad called me "Skeezics" (the cat?) or "Squeak" for a while but I'm not sure why, since it was long before my voice changed.

My sisters have always been very proud and supportive of their big brother, for which I remain duly grateful. I'm also very proud of them.

Cheney Grove

I was born at home in 1942, amid a small neighborhood of seven families in a grove of trees a mile from the center of Fort Fairfield, just off the Caribou Road. Cheney Grove was a wonderful place to grow up—a virtual paradise.

Besides my family there were our landladies, Bessie and Vastale Cheney, downstairs; the Gordon Glews next door; Joe Debay, with wife, daughters Doreen and Myrna, and son, Freddie; Chick Dewley and wife; the Pelletiers, with twin daughters Jean and June; and a Mr. Turner, who, I think, was replaced by a utility worker from Castle Hill who had a small boy, Mark. We all got along well and supported one another.

Cheney Grove was truly paradise, as far as I'm concerned. There was plenty to do there, with abundant raspberries and strawberries; hazelnuts in the woods; a tree stand and Tarzan swing in the deep part; a camp built by the older Glew boys and their friends; trout fishing in Hochenhull Brook beyond the trees and over Alton Clark's fields; the Bangor and Aroostook Railroad beyond the board fence; and the skeleton of Lester Cheney's abandoned Model A Ford, by which we traveled the world in our imagination. All day and into the evening we played pick-up ball, red light, statue, mother may I, marbles, tag, oly oly over, and other games long forgotten.

In winter we built forts and snowmen and went "sliding" across the tracks on White Hill. That's where I got my first black eye, trying to get too close and colliding with that cute Maggie MacDonald, an older girl. We all made big circles with crossed paths in the snow and played fox and geese, a kind of tag inside the lines. Sometimes Dad drove a huge orange snowplow for the town, brought it home at night, and created rounded snow banks for our tunnels and forts.

We didn't have a lot of toys, and we didn't need them—just a "toot-tee-too." As Jackie Gleason once explained, that's the leftover cardboard center of a toilet paper roll, which you put up to your mouth and say, "Toot-tee-too!"

Actually, we had a lot more than that, largely dependent on our imagination. I sneaked out of a nap one afternoon to sew my own carpenter apron like Dad's. I tried making spikes in the sides of my shoes like the local lineman but that didn't work out. I spent a lot of time trying to pull burdocks out of the ground with my tricycle while spinning the wheels in mud puddles. It didn't work but it was a lot of fun playing grownup. Nor did the skis work that I made out of barrel staves and tried out on a gravel driveway after the first few flakes of snow. I fell and hurt my knee on a rock, and it was clear from then on that skiing was not for me.

Life wasn't all fun and games. I had to shovel snow off the steps to our upstairs apartment, keep a clear path to the outhouse about 100 feet away, and empty the upstairs "piss pail" there every day, especially in winter. The roof of the outhouse was really convenient for eating chokecherries right off the high bushes in summer. It was said that you would get sick if you drank milk afterward, but I never tried to find out. We often used kerosene lanterns at night, and for years I sat at the table on a nail keg covered with cloth and cotton

David on the Glews' tire swing

17

padding on top.

Nevertheless, I spent my first nine years there happy and safe in a sheltered world.

Cracker

When I was quite young, I fell down the full length of the 2nd-floor stairs outside the Cheney house. Mom came running to see if I was all right. I said I was, so she asked why I was crying.

"I broke my cracker," I sobbed.

A similar thing happened to my middle sister, Cheryl. While we were trick-or-treating at Joe Debay's, she leaned against an unlatched door, fell down the stairs into the dark cellar, and knocked herself out. I had to run home and get Mom. Within a few minutes Cheryl came to and has been all right since. Or has she?

We knew not to waste food or to get our "good" clothes dirty. One of the few fights I mustered the courage to enjoin came at school when my personal bully, Gilbert Bossie, pushed me down and soiled my new pants. That was it. I knocked him down and began pummeling him for the first time. Suddenly realizing what I had done, I was glad to see Freddie Glew there to protect me, in case Gilbert got up to do me in. He

didn't, nor did he ever bother me again.

That reminds me of a favorite cartoon of the kid standing in a guy's soup at the next table and his mother saying, "I hope you're not getting your new pants dirty." We would never do that, of course, but if we did, that would be Mom's first thought. The second would be to "snatch us bald-headed."

We were part of the "Quiet Generation," according to my Belfast friend and fellow author, William Webb. That's the little-known crop of kids born between 1930 and 1944, in the shadow of the Depression and World War II, after the Greatest Generation and before the Baby Boomers. Bill wrote a wonderful book, *Happy Days Along the KENNEBEC*, about growing up in Hallowell, Maine. He perfectly captured and described in detail the way we grew up, just as Jean Sheppard's Ralphie in *A Christmas Story* parallels my life at Cheney Grove. I highly recommend Bill's book, if you want to know what a young boy's day-to-day life was like then in small-town Maine.

The Quiet Generation is the perfect moniker for the way my sisters and I grew up. Kids were supposed to be seen and not heard, so we were. We behaved in public, never caused scenes in stores, and did very little to call attention to ourselves in social settings.

In fact, when some of our more active cousins seemed a little wild to us, we would think, "What's wrong with them?"

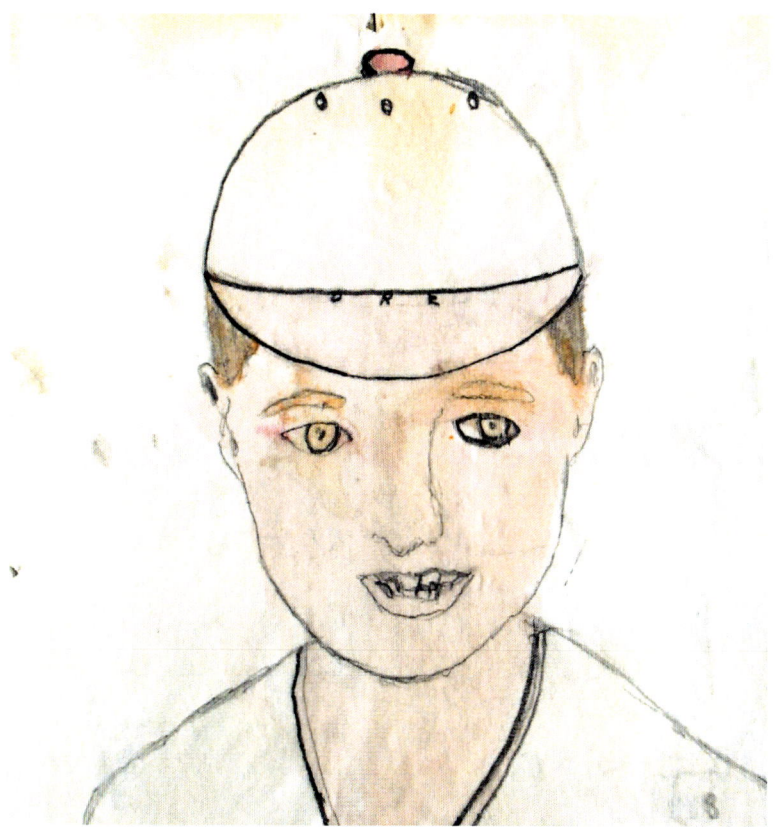

Self Portrait Age 8, 1950 graphite and watercolor, 4 ½" x 4 ½"

Budding Artist

My art career didn't start out very well. I was about five and trying to reproduce in the dirt at Cheney Grove what cousin Wayne had taught me the day before. Along came our landlady, the very staid Vassi Cheney. Uncharacteristically, she stopped to ask what I was doing.

"I'm making a pig's ass," I explained.

Well, she immediately flew upstairs to tell my mother the kind of talk I was having over (as they used to say). I guess my parents were surprised and amused, but I don't recall any repercussions. The whole subject of my dirt drawing, by the way, was "a bird's-eye-view of a pig's ass in the moonlight," which I can still do today. It was all Wayne's fault.

Once I got in Mrs. Libby's third-grade class at the Hacker School and was asked to draw pictures about stories we'd read, I was hooked. At the end of the year, my drawings were lining the walls above the chalkboards around the room, and it took her a long time to take them down. They included colored drawings of a family trip to coastal Maine that year. What a great boost to my confidence and a huge incentive to keep at it!

Shoe

As a small boy, I had the reputation of not always being in the here and now. In fact, for a while one family nickname for me was Dave Booby. I remember one incident that probably contributed to that name.

Late one afternoon, when I was around six or seven, I was making my way back up the path from the B & A Railroad's roundhouse to our home in Cheney Grove. As I got to the board fence, built to stop drifting snow, I heard someone calling my name in the distance. I looked up and saw Dad on the porch of our second-floor rental in the Cheney house. He was hollering something. "David, David," he kept calling.

I finally answered, "What?"

"Where's your shoe?" he asked.

I looked down and saw that everything seemed to be in order, so I answered, "It's on my foot."

"The other foot," he shouted.

Sure enough, I had only a sock on the other foot. With no idea what had happened, I thought I had better retrace my steps. I went back to the railroad yard and found the other shoe down in the roundtable circle.

Freddie Glew had recently shown me how to climb down there and how to get out. I had bravely tried it on my own that day, without Fred as a backup. I guess I was worried about whether I could get out of there, so I hadn't noticed that a shoe came off.

Freddie Glew

Freddie Glew was my next-door neighbor in Cheney Grove and my boyhood hero. He was two years older than me, the tenth of eleven children, and was everything I was not. For his age, he was the toughest kid I knew. He could run faster than anyone else, shinny up a tree faster, hit a ball or throw a rock farther and more true, excel at sports, and more than hold his own in a fight.

The Gordon and Mary Glew family was a great bunch. Gordon Junior had deep dimples and was always laughing. He loved to tease his sister, "Bug" (Jane Ann), who was wheelchair bound, to the point that she would bellow like a calf, whereupon Mrs. Glew would scold, "For God's sake, Junior, will you leave that kid alone?"

Freddie Glew

Junior told me one time that I should stay for supper. I asked what they were having and he told me it was "a thousand little things." It sounded interesting so I went home next door and asked Mom. She asked what they were having, and I said, "a thousand little things." She wanted to know what that was, so I went back and thanked Mrs. Glew, said I would stay, and asked what she was having.

"Baked beans," she answered.

I had a crush on Diana Glew and once made and hung a May basket for her. She sometimes babysat for us and could be tough, but her older sister, Marilla, was a real sweetheart, also with big dimples. Two older brothers, Mike and Willis, were great guys too. Perhaps because Fred and I were two boys close in age in a small neighborhood, we spent a lot of time together, playing "oly oly over" (throwing a ball to one another over his barn), baseball after supper, marbles, jackknife, playing Tarzan in the woods, throwing rocks, and fishing for trout at Hockenhull Brook. Fred was better than me at all of those things.

On more than one occasion, he came to my aid when a school bully decided to pick on me. His prowess did disappoint me once when he hit my sister Barbara in the throat with a rock because she insisted on following us when we were going fishing. I think he just meant to scare her, but his aim was just too sure. I remember only one case when I might have been better at something than Fred. I sensed that he didn't like coloring as much as I did and didn't stay inside the lines as well. As a mature artist, I now appreciate the creative value of not being so restricted.

Fred is still a hero in my mind today, and we have remained distant but good friends over the years.

Trains

The Bangor and Aroostook Railroad was between the Grove and town. It was the source of endless fascination, especially the big steam engines.

The B & A had a railway station, roundhouse, roundtable, potato-house sidings, track switches, boxcars, coal cars, flatcars, cabooses, and steam engines. We used to walk the rails all the way to Demerchant's store at the end of Depot Street, play in the roundtable circle, explore leftover contents of the boxcars, and climb all over everything. We collected railroad spikes, bottles, and loose change that winos sometimes lost on the tracks. We shouldn't have, but we sometimes put a coin on the tracks to watch it get flattened by a train. We could put an ear down on the rail and tell whether a train was coming.

At one point, Dad performed maintenance on the steam engines at night, getting them ready for the trip back to Bangor next day. After my sisters were asleep, Mom and I would sometimes walk down to the roundhouse, and I would climb up into the train cab with Dad. He let me shovel coal into the firebox and ride out onto the roundtable with him so we could turn the engine around and head it for Bangor. I knew that was someplace around the distant curve and about as far away as I could imagine. When the diesel engines replaced steam during the 1950s, they weren't nearly as impressive to a young boy.

Cold Cocked

I was talking to Dad one time about how some bosses could be complete jerks. He agreed and told me about one in his past, whom I won't name.

Dad was working at the time in the B & A roundhouse, just down the path from our home in Cheney Grove. He was late for work because he had rushed Mom to the hospital in childbirth with one of my sisters, probably the youngest, Alana. When he got to the job, his boss berated him for not being there on time. Dad tried to explain but to no avail.

"I don't care if she was having a kid or what she was doing," his boss said. "You're supposed to be here on time!"

"So I cold cocked the ignorant bastard," Dad related.

He "got done" right after that, as they say in Maine.

David and Daniel

Dad told this story of his visit to Mom when she was in the hospital.

A French Canadian woman was in the next bed, and her husband and twin boys had come in to see her. After a while, the young boys got restless and began chasing one another around the room. The father became annoyed with them.

"David," he said sternly. Both boys kept on running.

"Daniel," he said even more sharply. They didn't even slow down.

He turned to his wife in frustration and said, "Jeez Chrise, what dat kid's name?"

Road Work

Dad had a couple of other jobs that were impressive to a young boy. When he worked for the town, he sometimes drove a big, long road grader in the summer. He took me to work with him one Saturday while he graded the gravel shoulders of the Green Ridge Road. He let me steer it a few times that day, and it was a great thrill.

In the winter, Dad drove a big, orange snowplow called an Oshkosh. It was far bigger than the other plow trucks and you could barely see over the front plow. It had a wing plow that was lowered to push the snow farther off to the side of the road or create a half bank that helped keep drifting snow out of the main roadway. He took me plowing with him sometimes, and that too was a big thrill.

After I got interested in drawing, I asked Dad to draw me a snowplow, thinking he could do anything. I was really impressed that he took out his mechanical pencil and did a detailed drawing of the plow, complete with all the bolts. I thought it was a remarkable drawing. I realize now that he could do it because he really knew the subject.

Scary Stuff

One of my most frightening childhood experiences came from hearing about the movie *Frankenstein*, starring Boris Karloff and playing at the Paramount Theater at the Fort, as residents called the Town.

I was in the third grade or so and was outside the home of my friend, Gary Demerchant, near the end of the bridge, listening to him and another pal, Tom Gagnon, talk about this new movie monster. The monster had been dead but was brought back to life when electricity was sent through two spikes still in his neck. He was extra tall, had a square head with the top sown back on, and had dead-looking eyes with heavy lids. It was hard for me to imagine a scarier creature. As it started to get dark, I left with my bike and headed up the Caribou Road toward home in Cheney Grove.

I was doing fine until I turned up the Grove road and caught my pants leg in the bike chain. No matter what I did, I couldn't get it out. As it got darker and darker, I imagined all kinds of scary creatures in the dancing shadows of a pile of burning potato tops out in Alton Clark's field. I was close to panic and tears, expecting to be out there all night, when a neighbor, Joe Debay, turned up the road, saw me in his lights, and helped me out of my predicament. I was very grateful.

The next scary incident came as a nightmare after I saw the movie *The Thing*, with scenes that stayed in my mind for years. I had gone to see it with cousin Wayne and stayed overnight with him at Gram's. I don't know what I was dreaming but I thought something was coming to get me through the moving curtains of the open window, so I suddenly screamed, "Throw it out the window! Throw it out the window!"

Wayne sat bolt upright and said, "Throw what out the window?"

"The curtain," I said again. "Throw it out the window!" Then I finally woke up to realize it was just a bad dream.

The last scary experience that still stands out in my mind was hearing Alfred Hitchcock's *The Birds* on the radio late one night in Presque Isle, in the early 1950s. Dad was working late and Mom had sent us upstairs to bed, but I could still hear the program on the radio downstairs. Neither of us knew what we were about to hear. When those birds attacked and made it into the house, it was a lot scarier on radio than in the later movie, probably because you were left to your own imagination as to how horrible the attack could be. It also may have affected me more because I had all kinds of wings from game birds Dad had shot pinned to my wallpaper, along with pictures of bears and other wild animals from *Field & Stream* magazine.

Roy and Dale

Like a lot of kids in the 1940s, Barb and I thought we were Roy Rogers and Dale Evans.

It must have started from going to the movies Saturday afternoons. We would walk the mile on our own—down the path from Cheney Grove, onto the B &A tracks, past Demerchant's, Armstrong's and Donaghy's grocery stores and the hospital to Presque Isle Street, and down Main Street to the Indian trail. There were actually two trails, upper and lower, through the woods along Fort Hill and along the back street from the post office to the fire/police station, which was right across from the Paramount Theater. Two trails were handy in case we ran into Rubberneck Robinson, who was probably harmless but looked tall and scary. We were inspired by the Saturday matinees, usually westerns and often featuring Roy and Dale, who were great role models in the simplistic world of good and bad. We became them on the Indian trail, all the way back home and throughout the week until the next Saturday, and often sang the movie's theme song. I was particularly fond of "Carolina Moon."

We also played Roy and Dale to and from the Hacker School. One particular woodpile beside a potato house near the feed mill became the sheriff's office. We climbed up there every day to see if the sheriff had anything for us to do. Inevitably we had to round up a couple of bad guys for him before trudging off to school. It was the same on the way home.

A funny thing happened over 50 years later. Barb had flown down to Carolina to help us drive two vehicles back to Maine. As we were leaving a farewell party of our artist friends, the group spontaneously broke into song, singing Roy Rogers's theme song "Happy Trails to You." Since they didn't know our history, it was surprisingly appropriate and poignant.

Saturday Afternoon Movies

In the 1940s and early 1950s, most kids in town went to the movies Saturday afternoons. They were a bargain at 12 cents.

We got to see *News of the World*, a cartoon, maybe a short subject, a serial segment ending in a cliff-hanger for next week, previews of coming attractions, and two feature films (often westerns). Roy Rogers and Gene Autry were favorites, but we often saw Hopalong Cassidy, Whip Wilson, Lash Larue, Randolph Scott, Johnny Mack Brown, Durango Kid, Allen "Rocky" Lane, Red Ryder, or the Lone Ranger. Sometimes we would see Abbott and Costello or the Bowery Boys. Short subjects often featured Laurel and Hardy, the Little Rascals, or the Three Stooges.

All of this was in black and white, with a strong moral message. The difference between bad and good was very clear, and bad didn't pay. I'm sure this all had an important influence on how we see the world even today.

It wasn't just about the movies: there was the popcorn and candy too. Popcorn was 10 cents and candy bars or soda only five cents. An all-day sucker could last the whole afternoon. Prepackaged ice cream may have been 15 cents. People actually clapped, cheered, and threw popcorn into the air for a happy ending. Most kids walked to the theater and walked back home, with no threat of harm.

Santa

When I was seven or so, I got a call from Santa Claus on Christmas morning. You can imagine my surprise and delight.

Actually, it was "Voscar," a well-known Presque Isle photographer who had a show on WAGM radio doing the voice of Donald Duck. Some time earlier, I had sent him a drawing of Donald, and he had sent me back an autographed picture with a nice compliment. I also got a second Santa call from Uncle Wendell, Mom's brother.

Fifty years later in North Carolina, Karen and I had decided to skip Christmas, since we were far from home, no family was coming, and we didn't want to bother with a tree and decorations just for a week or two. Christmas morning we were up in the studio working on something and feeling a little strange about

Santa & Mrs. Claus, circa 1999 pastel, 12" X 18"

our decision when the phone rang and I picked up.

"Merry Christmas, David. Ho, ho, ho. Do you know who this is?"

"Santa," I exclaimed excitedly. It was a wonderful surprise. Santa and Mrs. Claus (the only way they were known in the area) had posed for a group of artists at Art 1 Gallery in Gastonia, and I had done a really good double portrait of them in pastel, but I didn't know them and hadn't seen them since. It was that Santa. Not long after the call, we were leaving Carolina and the Gallery gave me a goodbye exhibit of portrait drawings I'd done of many local residents. The Gallery wouldn't take any commissions, so I offered my pieces at one quarter of the usual price, hoping that many friends might want the drawings I did of them. Many people did. It was a great opening. Some of my nude models came over from Charlotte. They bought pieces and I gave them some. Santa and Mrs. Claus came too and bought the double portrait I had done of them. The Gallery took in and paid me over $3,000 that night.

Ten years later, back in Maine, we got for Christmas a photo of Elias, our honorary grandson and son of our honorary daughter, Carla Kull, and her husband, Jim. Elias was sitting on Santa's lap back in North Carolina and, you guessed it, Santa was the one I had drawn so many years before.

Cousin Wayne

As a youth, I was quite influenced by my many uncles, aunts, and cousins. On my father's side, cousin Wayne was right at the top.

Joseph Wayne Estey is the son of Dad's sister Alda, but was raised by my grandparents. He is two years older than me and was like my older brother growing up. I frequently stayed overnight at Gram's so we could do things together.

Wayne often figured things out before I did, so he taught me about cool clothes, the difference between us and girls, the latest music, and other things. Early on, we played, roughhoused, fished or "swam" in Libby Brook, or played wolfman around Gram's lilac bush with Gerald "Jeddo" Flannery and the Paradis boys, David and Dickie. We sometimes went to the pool or roamed around town. We loved going to movies and went to a lot of them, sometimes the same one many times. Wayne could talk Gram out of movie money just so she'd be rid of us.

I especially liked going over there around Christmas, when we would scour the Montgomery Ward and Sears and Roebuck catalogs for the latest

gun and holster sets or other toys we might dream of getting. Wayne often picked out the best stuff and usually got it. I knew better and chose more modestly. There were no guarantees, of course, but things often worked out. It was also really good to be in a house that had a coal furnace below, warm floors, and hot-air registers when you came in with frozen feet. That alone made Christmas.

As we got older, we loved dreaming up important projects. One time we worked a week or two to clean out and refurbish the old chicken coop so we could have a clubhouse. Sometimes we went too far, like the time we found some silver paint powder in the barn, mixed it with kerosene, and painted everything in sight, including the wooden clothesline posts out in the yard. Grampy wasn't too pleased when he came home for lunch.

In the mid-1950s, Wayne and I both liked to draw and paint, so we did a lot of that together on Gram's dining room table, mostly western outlaws and car designs. As we each became teenagers, Wayne was one of the first in town to embrace the new rock & roll music and dress like Elvis Presley, with a red coat, black pants, white bucks, a ducktail haircut, and sideburns. I took to calling him El. He was a good drummer and he liked to practice to Little Richard records, because they were so fast. Before I left the Fort, I painted huge flames on the front half of his little black coupe. It looked like a meteor coming down the road.

Smoking

In our teens, Wayne tried to get me to smoke. I told him no. Dad had told me not to smoke, so I wouldn't. "Do you always do what your Dad tells you?" he asked incredulously.

"Yes," I told him. "Why wouldn't I?"

Years later, I learned that Dad had started smoking at age ten, he and Donald Sherwood, out behind the woodpile. Grampy, who smoked strong, unfiltered Lucky Strikes, caught Dad smoking after he had become a strapping teen. "I don't mind you smoking," he told Dad, "as long as you buy your own."

Not long after, following supper one night, Grampy spoke up and said, "Randy, let me have one of your smokes."

"I don't mind you smoking," Dad replied, "as long as you buy your own."

Quick as a flash, Grampy was up and around the table, put his hands on Dad's shoulders and "drove my ass right down through the wicker chair, and I couldn't get out," Dad recalled. "I had to hobble out of the room and figure out how to get out."

"Jesus, he was strong, you know," he added.

I didn't take up smoking until I came home from college and found my little sisters smoking, so I bummed one off them quite often. Later I even took up a pipe for a while, then eventually quit smoking altogether. I never really enjoyed it that much.

Uncle Cecil

In the early 1950s, my dad's younger brother, Cecil, was a good-looking bachelor, a ladies' man, still living at home at 45 Elm Street and working as a mechanic for Peterson's Garage, along with Jim McGrath and Phil Burtsell.

Gib Peterson was smart to hire former beauty queens, Betty Bubar and Carolyn Kimball, to pump gas. Although there were several choices of gas in town, a lot of guys preferred to fill up at Peterson's Texaco, for the added lift they got.

One time, I rode back to the Fort from Presque Isle with Cec, at night in a blinding snowstorm, so I could spend the weekend with Wayne. We could just barely see the tops of the telephone poles. "Can you see the road now?" he would ask periodically. I would tell him I couldn't and he would answer, "Neither can I," and keep pressing ahead. At one point, we were shocked to suddenly see two orange lights appear right above us, and we just missed hitting a snowplow. We could travel the 12 miles at only about ten miles an hour, but we finally made it.

Like the rest of the family, Cec had a good sense of humor, some odd expressions, and a way with a story. I remember the time Gram found a huge egg laid by a bantam hen. "Goodbye, asshole," was his reaction. Another time when something had not gone well, he said, "Wouldn't that make a dog's ass want to suck a lemon?" Gram was none too pleased with his language.

One of his best stories was about one of his motorcycle buddies, Sonny Hilyard, younger brother of Uncle Clarence, who married Mom's sister Glenda. Sonny was revered as a rebel by the kids around town for blatting his loud bike the full length of Main Street.

One summer Sunday, the bikers had ridden up to Madawaska Lake in the heat. When they arrived, there were a lot of girls along the shore. "Of course them bikes were red hot," Cec said, "and that lake was ice cold. Sonny hung back, revving his bike: vroom, vroom, vroom. All of a sudden he shot out over the end of the pier and way out into the lake, just to impress the girls, you know."

"That engine block split all to hell," he added, "and Sonny had to call Dan (his father) to come get the remains."

Uncle Rollie

Dad's youngest brother, James Roland, was perhaps the funniest one of all, with a quick comment, an off-color joke or two, and an infectious laugh. He looked like Dad but with more wavy hair, and he probably acted a lot like him too in sowing wild oats. He was a very attractive young man who could sit down at the organ and play a song by ear. I didn't see a lot of him over the years but he was always a lot of fun to be around when I did.

I hadn't seen Rollie for several years when he ended up recently in the Eastern Maine Medical Center in Bangor. I went to see him and was stunned to turn the corner and see my own, late father lying in the bed—same chin, eyes, white hair, Estey nose, mouth, and rugged, square-ish head. Rollie had been very stout for many years but now had lost a lot of weight and was the spittin' image of Dad about five years before he passed. Rollie is now convalescing at Leisure Garden Apartments in Presque Isle, with his wife, Faye.

Arthur and Inez

My mother's younger brother Arthur married my father's younger sister Inez, so they were my uncle and aunt no matter how you look at it.

When they were first married, they lived in a front room of our family rental at Cheney Grove. She used to comb and part my hair nicely then send me out to ask my parents, "Aren't I the best-looking little boy in town?" After she had her firstborn, Carl, she doted on him the same way.

Inez was very much a tomboy, very funny, and one of our favorite aunts. She always addressed any gathering as boys, as in "What's going on, boys?" My sister Barbara and I used to stop at their house on Columbia Street on our way to and from the Hacker School. She would make jokes, feed us "David's" cookies, and maybe sing a song, accompanied by her guitar. We called her Judy Canova, a funny and popular country singer of the day. Our whole family would go over there to listen to Hank Snow and Lefty Frizzell on their floor-model radio and record player, and, a few years later, to watch their new, grainy television.

Arthur did carpentry and a lot of projects for old

ladies around town, so he was gone a lot in his pickup, often coming in just for meals then heading out again. He didn't seem to have much time for kids because he worked long hours, but he liked my sisters a lot. At one point, he started working with my grandfather at the high school across the street and he drove a school bus. Late in life, when he was still doing odd jobs and painting houses, he took Inez along and let her climb the ladder, saying, "Get up there, Inez, and see what's going on."

Marketing

I learned one of my first lessons in marketing from Inez when she worked at the five and ten.

There was some item that just wasn't moving. Inez thought it was because it was too cheap and people assumed it wasn't any good, so she upped the price. People then began to snap it up.

I had a similar experience many years later when I worked at the Mooring Restaurant's dairy bar in Belfast. One of the hot sauces for sundaes was Plantation Nut. Nobody ordered it, probably because they didn't know what it was. I made a hand-lettered label calling it "peanut butter fudge." Soon it was selling like hotcakes and people loved it.

Cousin Carl

A rthur and Inez's son Carl Doughty is a double cousin and one of my favorites. He grew up used to getting what he wanted when he wanted it.

He is four years younger than me, but we spent a lot of time playing together as kids. He had all the best toys. He's a great guy and we have remained close over the years, but he is also the subject of many humorous family stories about his quick temper and the resulting consequences. In deference to him, I'll relay only one, because it is very revealing about him and my father.

On a road trip back from Plaster Rock, New Brunswick, probably from a Doughty family picnic at Uncle Luther's on the Tobique River, Inez announced to Dad that he would have to stop soon because little Carl was getting hungry. Dad was already annoyed at Carl for kicking the back of his seat, "right into my kidneys," the whole way. So he pulled into a country store and took everyone's order, including Carl's, for a plain hamburger with nothing on it, no tomato, no green stuff and no condiments – just the way he likes it to this day. When Dad returned and Carl inspected his hamburger, it included ketchup. He immediately "scaled" it out the open window into the woods, whereupon Dad jumped back into the car and sped home, without stopping again.

Years later, Carl loved to break into fits of laughter as Dad would retell the story and end with, "You're god-damned lucky you grew up, because I almost killed you that day."

Cousin Gerry

Gerry Driscoll, son of my dad's sister Cecilia and her husband, Jim, is one of the funniest people I ever knew. His quick wit and sense of humor is unmatched.

No one can tell stories like Gerry, and he has a lot of them. One of the funniest involved him and cousin Carl and a runaway soapbox-derby car on Presque Isle Street hill. Another was his getting up in the dead of night to go to shovel pea vines into the hopper at the nearby A & P processing plant. I won't even try to do justice to the stories here but, instead, will relay another incident of him in action that I actually witnessed.

It happened when I took Mom and her twin sister, Madeline Hansen, over to Celia's to visit my aged Grandmother Estey. In the course of the visit, Celia proudly produced a family photo of her and Jim, along with their three children, Gerry, Peggy, and Doug.

Madeline said, "I'd like to have a nice family picture taken of me and Earle, Billy, and Steven, but the boys have that cussed long hair and I'm almost ashamed of the way they look."

Gerry was quick with a solution. "Here's what you do, Madeline," he suggested. "Have a picture taken with you and Earle sitting on the couch with the boys standing behind it back to. Then you can proudly show it off: 'Here's me and Earle and the boys.'"

Cousin Mary

On second thought, I will relate one of Gerry's stories about our mutual cousin, Mary Bennett, the oldest child of Dad's sister Alda and Arnie Bennett. I'll try to convey it the way Gerry does.

Mary was between Gerry and me in age, a small, quiet girl who was apparently a lot tougher than I knew, according to him. He tells of finding that out as a kid when he ran into her at the top of the stairs in the Hopkins Block, where she was arguing with her boyfriend, who had made the near-fatal mistake of looking at another girl.

"All of a sudden she hauled off and knocked him ass over teakettle down the stairs to the second landing. Before he could get up, she was on him again, knocked him down the rest of the stairs and out cold, went down and stepped over him, then walked out into the street. Later on, as she was driving through town with her mother, she spotted the girl in question. She hollered for Alda to stop the car but jumped out while it was still rolling, ran up onto the sidewalk, and beat the livin' daylights out of that girl."

After that, Gerry says, he was scared to death of Mary and always crossed the street whenever he saw her coming. Today, Mary says he exaggerates to make her look bad. I think he does it to make a better story, but I don't doubt that Gerry, who has become a strapping man, was afraid of her in their youth.

Cousin Bill

Billy Hansen is the son of Mom's twin sister, Madeline. We were very close growing up and have remained so, but my most memorable story about Bill occurred in the early 1970s, when we were both adults.

I was living outside Baltimore when Bill called out of the blue to come rescue him from Washington. His hippie companion had dropped him off at a fleabag hotel a few blocks from the Capitol building while she went on to visit relatives in Virginia. I found him with long hair and a beard in a room crawling with cockroaches. When I brought him home, my first wife, Susie, made him take off all of his clothes before entering the house.

That weekend, we had long talks about where

he had been and where his life was going. I was very impressed that he could play guitar in about any style, be it Chuck Berry, Chet Atkins, or others. Susie and I tried hard to convince him that his relationship with this woman was going nowhere. By Sunday afternoon, we drove him to meet her in the parking lot of a local Washington area shopping center. They talked for a long time in her truck with a colorful box on the back, where apparently they had been living. Finally he got out, extracted his few belongings, and left with us. It must have been very difficult, but he did it.

He went back to Maine and, before long, married Mary (Giles), with whom he belongs. They had two great kids, Sarah and Matthew, and settled in Yarmouth. Besides his regular job, he continued his music and regularly played blues guitar in several venues around Boston and Portland, including the Portland Museum of Art. The CD "At Last," by Diana Hansen's Blue Willow band, including Bill, is among my very favorite music for painting. He retired and moved last year to Portland, OR to be closer to Sarah and Matt, who is also an accomplished blues guitarist.

Uncle Bud

On my mother's side, perhaps no one spent more time with me or had more influence than Uncle Bud.

Charles Maurice "Buddy" Doughty was my grandmother's youngest surviving child. She must have been exposed to a few things beyond the farm, for she named him after Charles Boyer, Maurice Chevalier, and Buddy Clark. She died in 1933, three years after his birth.

Bud had a strong will from the start and was impossible to keep in school. His father eventually gave up and let him stay at home, without learning to read or write, except for his name, address, and a few other words. Nevertheless, he grew up with the Doughty work ethic and had his own chores around the farm. He taught me to chop and stack wood properly. He emulated his older brothers in the service, and had his own helmet liner, MP arm patch, military fatigues and khakis, brass insignia, combat boots, billy club, and wooden rifle. Army clothes and boots were his mode of dress for many years. He was often quiet and stayed to himself, yet he was comfortable around his younger nieces and nephews, and great entertainment for them

Bud, 1961 graphite & ink, 15" x 10"

with his funny noises and odd sayings.

I remember how he used to pester his Aunt Louise Coes, whose father had been the driver for the famous racehorse, John R. Braden, for whom the Presque Isle movie theater was named. Bud would make a noise like a cat's meow and Louise would search the house in vain trying to find the animal.

Once he moved into town, "Charlie" became a well-known figure, mainly because he "tramped the streets," as everyone put it, doing odd jobs and serving as a carrier of mail, paperwork and other exchanges among the storeowners. He never let any moss grow under his feet, as he was always in a half run, as if he were on a mission—which he usually was. He did a lot of work for storekeepers Naz Gannam and Sawyer George, who outfitted him with a suit and hat of "very best quality." Years later, he went to work as a janitor for the Interstate Foods processing plant and actually retired from there at 65, with a pension.

Bud was very frugal and guarded his money. He ate very little over the years, usually just crackers and sardines, with coffee throughout the day. On a rare occasion he ate oyster stew or other favorites right out of the can, unheated so as to save on the electric bill. He was small of stature and rail thin, weighing only about 85 to 100 lbs. In his late years, he rented a small apartment, but he rarely bought material things to improve his lot. After he retired, he would hitch a ride to the Presque Isle Mall and back to spend the day hanging out, flirting with the store clerks, and accepting donations from generous strangers.

Unfortunately, Bud was hurt in an accident on one of those trips and didn't have enough reserve strength to recover. I felt very bad, as the poor little guy always fended for himself in his adult life and never did any harm to or wished it on anyone. Ironically, when he died at 71, after a life of extreme frugality, he was carrying $500 to $600 in his wallet, and he was the only one in the family who ever left thousands of dollars to his siblings or their children.

Connecticut

Bud used to collect matchbooks from all over the country that he found on the street. I think it was his way of connecting to the world outside of Fort Fairfield, Maine.

At one point, he got a chance to see some of that world during a visit to his sister Glenda and her husband, Clarence Hilyard, in Norwalk, Connecticut. Bud was certainly impressed. He came back bragging about how big everything was there, how much room there was, and how small everything was in Aroostook County.

I made the mistake of defending Aroostook and trying to put things into some perspective. I told him that Aroostook County was bigger than the state of Connecticut and that all of the other New England states could fit inside the state of Maine. I even pulled out maps to prove it to him.

Bud wasn't buying it. "The fellers that make them maps don't know anything. I been there, I seen it." End of conversation.

Bicycle

In my early teens, Bud and I used to make a lot of treks five miles out of town to the old homestead on the Sam Everett Road, through the woods, and across the Canadian border to visit Robert and Helen Clark. Aunt Helen was the sister most like Bud's mother in that she had 12 kids.

Usually we went on Thursdays when Helen made donuts or churned butter—meaning she'd have fresh buttermilk. We even went in the wintertime. In fact, one time we stayed too long and got caught in a brutally cold snowstorm on the walk back. We tried to cut across Loomie Bell's fields, but the snow there was almost to our waists. I thought we were going to freeze to death before we made it about four miles to Campbell's store in Puddle Dock to warm up.

In the summer, since I had access to a bicycle, Bud decided he needed one, so the trip to Canada would be a lot easier and faster. He heard somehow that Johnny Chambers, who lived across from the homestead, had an old bike, so we went out to take a look. It wasn't much, repainted a dull black (probably to hide the rust) but it worked, so Bud offered five bucks for it. Johnny accepted.

Not far from there on the way back, Bud caught his pants leg in the bike chain and couldn't get it out. We finally had to rip his pants to free him. Bud was hopping mad. He went up over the hill and found an axe in the old woodshed, then came back and chopped that bike all to hell, breaking the spokes and slitting the tires, and so forth. Then he dragged the bike back to Johnny and insisted he get his money back. Johnny complained that Bud had ruined it, but Bud insisted it was no good anyway.

Knowing how irrational and hard-headed Bud was, Johnny finally had the good sense to give in, take what was left of the bike, and give Bud his five bucks back.

Satisfied everything was finally fair and square, we went home.

Watermelon

One of the things Bud and I liked to do on a hot, boring summer day was walk the length of the CP Railroad tracks behind Main Street and pick up coins or bottles.

We got two cents each for soda bottles and one cent each for beer bottles, so by the time we got to the A & P supermarket, we had enough for a pint of ice cream or cottage cheese, which we both loved. We'd take our treat out back to share it in the shade.

One time we really hit the jackpot when we had enough change for a watermelon that had just arrived in the store. We bought it and took turns carrying it out back. In one of the transfers, we dropped it on the tracks and it split all to pieces. We hardly had time to react when a dozen kids came out of nowhere and gobbled up the juicy chunks. It was so amazing that we broke out into fits of laughter right then and every time we told of it thereafter.

Lunch Break

Bud was pretty set in his ways, as became quite clear when his brother Bruce took him to work with him at the lumberyard in Manchester, CT.

Around noon, Bud made clear it was time for lunch. Bruce said he wanted to finish the pile he was working on and then they would get something to eat. About fifteen minutes later, he finished up and they went to the local corner store. By then, Bud said he wasn't hungry and didn't want anything.

"What do you mean?" Bruce asked incredulously. "Fifteen minutes ago it seemed like you were starving."

"I eat at 12 o'clock," Bud said.

Funerals

Bud never liked funerals, or large family gatherings, for that matter. When we came back home for family reunions, Bud was nowhere to be found. The same was true when we had a funeral for his sister, Madeline Hansen, with whom he had lived for many years.

Afterward, I found him at his usual perch on the library steps, so I stopped to say hello. "Sorry about Madeline," he said. "I couldn't go. I was too busy."

"I know," I said. "You never liked funerals, anyway. In fact, I remember you always said you wanted us to throw you right in the river when you die, right?"

"Nope," he said.

"What do you mean?" I asked. "You always said that."

"I changed my mind," he said. "I can't swim."

Years before, Sam Bentley, one of Bud's neighbors, used to tell a story about the strangest funeral he ever went to:

"Say, the wife came in and sat way down front. Then the brothers came in and sat way down front. Then the sisters came in and sat way down front. Say, pretty soon, the corpse came in and sat way up back."

Two Good Men

Bud and I spent a lot of time together. He was 12 years older than me but younger in his mind, and we had a similar sense of humor. He was always full of foolishness, so he was very popular with all of his nieces and nephews.

Kennedys, 1966/67 oil, 24" X 36"

Perhaps because we did so much together or because I treated him like an older brother, I was one of his favorites. I also kept in touch with him, made and sent drawings and paintings of the Kennedys to him, got him an autographed picture of JFK, and always looked him up when I came back to the Fort. We would sometimes pick up a couple of cold beers at the store in Puddle Dock and head out the Sam Everett Road. I would ask what kind of beer he liked. "Beer's beer," he said.

A couple of years before he died, Bud paid me the ultimate compliment, through my father. Dad was back in town to see his mother and stopped in for a coffee at Lennie's, the only remaining restaurant in town. There, in a back booth, as usual, was Bud, having a cup of coffee. Dad went over and sat down to see if he could engage Bud in conversation, which often was not easy.

At one point, Bud looked Dad in the eye and said, "There are only two good men in the world, John F. Kennedy (who was assassinated many years before) and David Estey."

Dad didn't say where he thought that left him, or Bud, for that matter.

Uncle Bruce

Bruce Doughty was always grinning. He and Aunt Phyllis (Dorsey) were like two kids together their whole lives, so they were great fun to be around.

I didn't get to spend much time with Bruce growing up because they moved to Connecticut, but when he was around, we liked to stroll uptown and maybe grab a hotdog, which he loved. He always used to say he would have been taller but he wore his legs off dragging pails of water up to the farmhouse from the springhouse over the brook. Later on, there was a hand pump over the kitchen sink that had a long-handled dipper that everyone drank from and that crackled during lightning storms, but that was all too late for Bruce. Like his brothers, he was a funny guy, quick with a joke and a laugh. I especially remember one funny remark when I was already in my mid-forties, and he was, of course, a whole generation older.

We were leaving a gathering at Uncle Clarence Hilyard's in Spring Mount, Pennsylvania. I had walked out to the car with Bruce and remembered that I'd forgotten something. "See, Bruce, that's what happens when you get to be my age," I said.

"I'm not looking forward to it, I'll tell you that right now," he replied.

Uncle Earle

Earle Hansen married my mother's twin sister, Madeline.

According to Dad, Earle was a regular Huck Finn in his youth, with high-water pants, bare feet, and an ability to snag a trout out of Petty Brook with an alder switch, some string, a bent nail, and an angleworm. If there was a fish in there to be had, Earle was going to get it.

He served in World War II, like his many brothers-in-law. He came home, married, raised two sons, Billy and Steve, and worked as a plumber for Guy Belmain. He was a great husband, father, and uncle.

I saw a lot of him growing up, especially after the stores closed Saturday nights, when our family often went to Earle and Madeline's house for coffee and snacks. I remember him as a very quiet man who, on rare occasions, played the mouth organ or Jew's harp. Mostly he just followed the conversation by sitting back with his head turned slightly so as to view things from a sideward glance.

Karen and I were visiting years later and she was telling about the fierce thunderstorms she remembered growing up two miles out of Fort Fairfield on the windswept Center Limestone Road. "When the lightning got close and the thunder was really loud, Mother and Daddy would get us all up and we'd sit down in the middle of the hallway and wait it out," she explained.

Earle was sitting back, listening to all these stories without saying a word, until he finally came up with something her father might well have said in a slightly different way: "By Jeez, you ain't gonna outrun lightning."

Billy recently relayed one of his father's stories about his brother-in-law, Perley Henderson, who also was from the Sam Everett Road and was moaning and groaning of constipation from the steady diet of lumberjack food in the woods. When someone suggested a laxative, Perley said, "No sir. If you keep shoveling 'er in, she's got to come out."

Bill also told me one of Earle's expressions that I've never heard anywhere else: "I've got something caught in my hoozler"—meaning his throat.

Uncle Harry

During World War II, Harry Doughty guarded prisoners as an MP out in Arizona, I think. Afterward he came back and was one of the boys running the farm.

One time I was out with them in the front seat of the old, blue Dodge truck. Harry was distracted in his driving and ran into the back end of, I think, Frank Summerson's truck. I banged into the windshield and came out with a big bump on my head and a bad headache. They took me up to the farmhouse, put me down on the sofa in front of a small woodstove, put a cool towel on my head, and asked whether they could get me anything in town. Seeing a golden opportunity to cash in, I said I wanted five packs of Juicy Fruit gum. They dutifully complied. I was feeling much better when they got back.

Later, Harry married Mary Jamer, from across the border, and started a family. I went to their wedding and Barb was the flower girl. Aunt Mary was and remains a beautiful woman, inside and out. Harry went to work for Mrs. Stevens, running a feed mill near the B & A. It was a great place for him, and for me, as lots of funny stories and jokes were swapped on rainy days, when farmers came in to have feed ground and mixed. It gave Harry enough downtime to keep up with politics and make up a lot of ridiculous stuff, two loves that were probably not mutually exclusive. I loved spending time there, especially when I got big enough to help him out. He made up and even drew pictures of a lot of nonsensical characters, like "seebeelumps," which I don't remember ever seeing spelled out.

One time, somebody asked him if he wanted a kitten and he answered, "No, I haven't got a thing around here for a cat to do." By the way, he always claimed that the way to catch a mouse was to make a noise like a piece of cheese.

One time a bunch of us cousins were gathered around his table and Aunt Mary served peas. One of us dropped one and it rolled across the floor. "Jump on her," Harry said, to counter the embarrassment.

Uncle Ralph

I may have spent more time with Uncle Ralph than with the other Doughty boys, except for Bud, since Ralph ended up with the farm.

He had the same sense of humor as the others, but he was a lot quieter, so I don't have as many funny stories about him. Like them, he was in the military during the war and sent us letters and gifts. Afterward, he married Geneva Fraser and their first child, Marilyn, was one of my many cousins born in 1949 and the most beautiful little girl you can imagine.

I loved to be out on the farm with Ralph, especially on a rainy day, when we would work in the machine shed on the equipment, with the smell of gasoline and fertilizer mixed. Often we would have to go into town for a part, which gave us a chance to have a candy bar and a pop (soft drink). Geneva took care of Barb and me when Mom had Cheryl. She was very good to us, but she did one thing that I never liked: serving me a tall glass of fresh cow's milk at room temperature. I would gulp it down to be done with it, but she would immediately refill the glass.

One year, when "Santa Claus was very poor," as Dad put it, Ralph made me a roll-top desk and chair for Christmas. A few years later I used all of its pigeonholes to keep track of my digging money and expenditures, like Uncle Bud. It may have put me on the path to becoming a bureaucrat 15 years later.

Ralph liked fishing a lot more than farming, so in the early 1950s he dammed up the little spring-fed brook and stocked the resulting pond with trout. Before he could really enjoy it, Hurricane Carol wiped it out. Shortly thereafter he gave up the farm.

I remember one story of his quiet ways. In the 1960s he was telling some of us how congested the county seat of Houlton was getting. He had ventured down recently to the great metropolis (not much bigger than Fort Fairfield), and the traffic was so bad and his nerves so frazzled that he had to go to bed when he got home.

Uncle Rob

I didn't know Uncle Robert Doughty very well, even though for some years, we lived fairly close to him.

I remember him mostly as a very serious guy, driving through town in his pickup, chuck full of business, managing the crews doing work for Reed Brothers, the uncle and father of Governor John Reed, who'd been in my father's class. Later in life, Uncle Rob wrote two very informative books about the Doughty family, one called *Samuel Everett the Pioneer* and the other *My Life's Story in Aroostook County Maine*. They must be in the Fort Fairfield Library even today.

I never appreciated that Rob had a great sense of humor, like the younger Doughty boys, until the last time I took my mother to the Fort before she passed away. We were staying at the home of her twin sister, Madeline Hansen, on Currier Street. One by one, her brothers stopped by to keep us all in stitches. Surprisingly, Uncle Arthur, another busy and serious guy, was one of them. But then Rob stopped by.

One of his funniest comments was his reaction to news that Dad's sister Alda, and her husband, Gene Butler, both retirement age, had gone down to the coast to rake blueberries. Suggesting that they readily would take on any kind of job to make a few extra bucks, he joked, "That Alda and Gene could rake a hayrack full of blueberries before lunch."

To appreciate how nonsensical that is, you have to envision how big and porous a ribbed hayrack is and how impossible it would be for it to contain little blueberries.

Uncle Walter

As a kid, I loved to run around with Uncle Walter Doughty. He and Aunt Verna (Hansen) never had children but they loved kids, and Walter almost always had one with him. After me, there was a long string of younger cousins. He and Verna left their house to a care-giving nephew.

Walter was like a kid himself in many ways, and he was very generous. He loved Tom and Jerry cartoons and comic books. He had a sweet tooth and always had lots of candy and soda pop around. He liked a piece of hard candy after smoking his pipe. He also liked to take time out for a nap in the afternoons, whenever he could. I'm with him there. I think the world would be a lot better off if everyone did.

As one of the older Doughty boys, Walter had his serious side. In World War II, he fought under General MacArthur at Guadalcanal and was wounded. As a dyed-in-the-wool Republican, he was like his father and most people in Maine at the time. He hated President Truman for firing the General, just as his father had hated Roosevelt. Like his brothers in the service, he had sent presents and letters home to me before I was old enough to read them. Afterward, the war and the army were never far from his thoughts, and he wore army fatigues for many years as a civilian. He liked to pull out maps and talk about his experiences, and he stayed interested in national politics. He became a professional bricklayer and did a lot of work on Loring Air Force Base in Limestone.

Like many of the Doughtys, Walter had a quick temper when work didn't go well. Dad once told me of the time he was working with some of the brothers and they had trouble with the truck, probably the old green International on the doors of which Uncle Wendell had painted "Doughty Brothers" in white. In the process of trying to get the distributor cap off, Walter skinned his knuckles and promptly scaled the part way off into the woods. The others stood there aghast, realizing it was getting dark and there was no way to drive without it. One of them walked all the way back to the farmhouse for flashlights, and they spent a good while searching through the puckerbrush to find the thing so they could drive home. It was a long day.

I'm sure Walter didn't think of the consequences at the spur of the moment, but I understand how good it must have felt to "whoop and drive it" into the woods.

Uncle Wendell

Wendell Doughty was always fascinating to me, not just because he had two thumbs on one hand (his mother wouldn't take one off when he was an infant because she didn't want to hurt him), but also because he was a talented artist.

When my first little dog, Trixie, a beagle, ran away from Cheney Grove, Wendell carved a beagle for me, and I still have it, along with a couple of eagles. He carved a lot of such items over the years, as well as miniature potato barrels and seed racks. He also was an accomplished sign painter who painted farm names and logos high up on barns throughout the township. I often went with him on those jobs and marveled at his skill. Some say I got my artistic bent from him, but my mother and her twin sister also used to draw and paint pretty well. I have a very detailed pencil drawing of Tom Mix that Mom drew and a painting of Snow White she did in house paint on glass. Aunt Madeline painted Snow White and all seven dwarfs on glass.

Wendell was the next-to-the-youngest Doughty and served in Japan during World War II. Like his brothers, he sent back gifts and letters to his nephew and niece. Much of his life he was what my father-in-law would call a "cowman," in that he tended the dairy cows for Barnes Brothers on the West Limestone Road. I loved to go out there, to stay overnight with him and Aunt Lorraine and hang out with him. He knew all the cows by name and they responded to him. So did the prize-winning bull, Cossar Hillman—most of the time. That bull was so strong that he once raised the front of a John Deere tractor chained to his nose. Years later, when I was home from college and living in Belfast, I drove over to the Skowhegan Fair to sleep overnight in the stalls with Wendell and the cows. He always took an interest in my artistic development.

Probably because of Wendell, our family picked potatoes for Barnes Brothers the three years I was in grammar school, and I first met my wife, Karen. I also met a very memorable picker, Mrs. Bradford, and her family. She was very thin, with a long neck, and reminded me of Popeye's girlfriend, Olive Oil. When I described her to cousin Freddie Clark one Saturday night, he seared her into my memory by quipping, "Her neck is so long she has to stand on a chair to blow her nose."

That's the kind of nonsense all the Doughty boys would appreciate.

Kay and Elbert

My family loved to make the long summer trip from the Fort down to Palmyra, ME to visit Aunt Kay, my mother's oldest sister, and Uncle Elbert Fields.

Kay's home was a fun and generous place, and we enjoyed playing with the two cousins around our age, Rachel and Rita. It was worth the long and hazardous 200-mile trip on gravel roads, often involving a flat tire or two. We had to pass through the lonesome 75 miles of Haynesville woods, made famous by Fort's own Dick Curless in his hit recording of "A Tombstone Every Mile." Another of my close cousins, Madeline's son, Bill Hansen, is an excellent bass guitar player who performed with Dick for a while and is on his *Maine Train* album.

Kay was a big woman with a big heart, but she was also the disciplinarian if she thought we were getting a little too active. One time when she asked us to sit, quiet down, and stay put, Elbert had just come in from his garage, so he made his usual contribution with a knowing wink and this advice: "Don't you move an inch."

That was typical of Elbert, who spent long hours under cars on the dirt floor of his auto repair shop. He often got help from his daughter "Min" (Lois), who was an attractive tomboy and perhaps the most like him. Apparently he was a very good mechanic for a long time, until the new cars came out with electronic components. He even worked on Governor (later Senator and then Secretary of State) Ed Muskie's car after it broke down nearby. As I understand it, Muskie always took his car to Elbert after that.

Kay and Elbert had a big barn with a cow, a big garden, and a field of beans, where I learned to do the back-breaking job of picking them. Cousin "Bubby" (Dana) taught me how to milk the cow. I slowly got a half pail on my own one time before she kicked it over, so I milked her again. Bub was often full of song and dance—like Uncle Bud in many ways. He was also my inspiration to go to college, as very few in our family had. Later, I was the best man at his wedding. The boss of my Pittsfield cousins was the oldest one, Shirley, who later worked for many years at and retired from the Bangor Library. We've all remained close.

Presque Isle

When I was entering the 4th grade, we moved 12 miles from Fort to Presque Isle, where Dad and his brothers Cecil and Rollie started Estey's Texaco Service Station, on Main Street, across from the city pool.

We rented a house from Jim and Skippy Carroll at 15 Pleasant Street, four or five houses up from the recreation center. It was the coldest house we ever lived in. The only heat came from a kerosene cook stove in the kitchen, and there was no heat source upstairs. In winter we had to take a hot water bottle to bed, keep on our socks and "union suits" (long underwear), and hurry downstairs in the morning. There was a shower upstairs, but in winter, we took baths downstairs, standing in a basin behind the kitchen stove.

When we moved in, the property had a fascinating barn with split-door horse stalls. It immediately became my "office" and clubhouse, but not for long. It was torn down and replaced with a new but boring shed. Even so, I used it to keep my jugs of frog eggs, so I could watch them turn into tadpoles then frogs.

I soon developed several good friends: Carroll

Cub Scout troop in Presque Isle, David, Chris Holmes, Carroll Carvell, Jimmie Richie, Tommy Holmes & Ernie Britton

Carvell, Richie Green, Tommy Holmes, and Danny Beaulieu. Richie was perhaps the most outgoing and the natural leader. Although he was sometimes a little aggressive, he was a good friend. His father owned a clothing store on Main Street. Carroll was a little younger and an all-around good guy. Tommy was a natural Boy Scout; his parents became leaders of our Cub Scout pack. Danny was a bit of a braggart but a nice guy. His father, "Spike," owned a grocery on Chapman Street. Sadly, one of my friends up the street, "Beanjuice" Bray, hanged himself as a young boy, for some unknown reason. On a happier note, a very nice Air Force couple moved in next door, and their beautifully dimpled daughter, Nancy Connors, became a good friend. We exchanged graduation pictures many years later.

We boys did all the usual guy things in summer, but in winter we spent a lot of time at the recreation center or playing war outside on the snow banks, since this was the time of the Korean Conflict. Richie was especially occupied with military matters, making models of P-36 conventional aircraft and the new F-86 Sabre jets. I tried to make them but didn't do well and couldn't afford it. When the weather was warmer, we liked to go out to the edge of Presque Isle Air Force Base and watch sabre jets take off and land.

My fourth grade teacher in Presque Isle, Miss McLane, was a nature enthusiast and inspired students to be, as well. In a Cub Scout project for our den mother, Mrs. Holmes, I drew a book of birds in color. After that, I just kept going, drawing more birds, animals, dinosaurs, fossils, and prehistoric rock formations. I was producing so many drawings that I enlisted Barb to color them for me.

We all went to the Training School in the 4th grade. It was there that I mustered enough courage to be on stage and, as Tiny Tim, utter my only line, "God bless us all, every one." In 5th grade we went to the Normal School (now University of Maine at Presque Isle—UMPI), where student teachers Mr. Carter and Mr. Bouchard were very supportive. George Bouchard passed away in May 2014. In 5th grade, I developed a crush on Barbara White, who lived down on Chapman Street, near my friend Royce Farrington.

Fudge

Carroll Carvell came over one night when I was babysitting the girls. I think it was his idea to make fudge.

We were doing fine until Carroll misread the recipe and replaced a cup of sugar with salt. We tried our best to drown it out with more bitter cocoa and sugar, until we ran out of sugar. The result was way too salty and way too bitter, but it cooked up nicely and, unlike Mom's, it was moist but nice and solid too.

She and Dad weren't impressed when they got

home. Barb and I had to eat all of it over the next week, as we knew better than to waste food. Carroll got off scot-free.

Danny Beaulieu

Danny Beaulieu used to stop by our Pleasant Street home on the way through the backyards and past the house of Dick Graves (now a prominent local doctor and historian) to the Training School. One morning, Danny had an unbelievable story to tell.

It was bitter cold that day, but every winter day seemed bitter cold in that house, with only the kitchen kerosene stove for heat and frost on the inside walls that we scraped off with our fingernails on the way downstairs to breakfast. We were complaining about how cold it was in the house that morning, but Danny, as usual, had to be one up on us.

"That's nothing," he said. "My mother left the refrigerator door open all night and it was forty below in our house this morning."

Funny Books

As a kid, I loved comic books, or funny books, as we called them. They cost only ten cents, but we usually ended up trading them with our family and friends.

I got my early literary education from funny books, not real books, even getting an inkling of the classics through them. I didn't care much for the silly cartoon characters like Porky Pig or Tom and Jerry. I liked Superman, Captain Marvel, Wonder Woman, and especially Plastic Man. I also liked scary stuff like Frankenstein, the Mummy or alien invaders, who were mild by today's standards. When *Mad* magazine came out, that was a special inspiration.

In sixth grade, at the Cunningham School in Presque Isle, I found two like minds in Danny Everett and Walter Christie. We all liked comics and we liked to draw. At some point, we each started to produce our own comic books, poking fun at the day's events, celebrities, and our own lives and friends at school. *Mad* magazine was our guide. One of us would come out with a book of a dozen pages and pass it around to the other two. A few weeks later another of us would come out with his. We did that throughout the school year. I wish we still had them today, but I guess not. I've reconnected with Danny but not Walter.

In the fall of that year, with money from picking potatoes for Harold Carmichael, I took turns treating my sisters, Barbara and Cheryl, to a Saturday night out. We would first go to the Rexall drugstore on Main Street for a hot fudge sundae and a half hour or so of sitting on the floor reading our favorite comics off the rack. Then we would go across the street to the John R. Braden Theatre, named after a racehorse, for a movie, complete with popcorn and candy. It was a perfect evening in my mind, but Cheryl got sick from too much stuff on one outing.

I never really got much into reading books until I had Mrs. Elsie Boynton for an English teacher at Crosby High School in Belfast. I loved her and she was the first one to tell me I could write.

I liked living in Presque Isle, but there was a longstanding sports rivalry with Fort, and I still felt a certain loyalty to my original hometown. After three years, Dad's business failed, in part because a lot of airmen ran up credit, got reassigned, and left without paying. In the summer of 1954, we moved back to the Fort.

62 Below

Winters in Aroostook were very cold and dry, with temperatures 30 degrees below zero not uncommon. Once it got that cold, you couldn't tell how cold it was, except your nose got red or even white on the end (frostbite) much more quickly.

One particular morning, after we had moved back to the Fort and I was in the 7th or 8th grade, it was especially cold. The thermometer outside our door read 62 degrees below zero. I walked to school that day, only about a block from our rental over the Hersey garage on Main Street, up the hill and past Foster's service station. My hands got so cold I couldn't unbutton my coat. Miss Stevens had to help me. How she got there from the other side of town I never knew, because no vehicles started in town that day. Later we learned that it was officially 60 below at the Caribou weather station. Very few kids showed up for school that day, but we held classes. Miss Stevens was probably our oldest teacher, as she had also taught my dad. The whole thing reminded me of another teacher Dad once had.

When he was going to the one-room Stevensville School out on the Caribou Road, he had another dedicated and elderly teacher, Lucy Sullivan. She lived farther from the school than Dad and had to pass his place to get there.

As Dad used to tell, when it snowed hard, he and his siblings kept a sharp eye out on the road, hoping she wouldn't make it and there would be no school. More often than not, sooner or later, "a little black speck would appear way off over the distant hill," and their hearts would sink. As it got closer, it became clear that there was going to be school, "come hell or high water"—or deep snow, as the case would be.

Law Enforcement

Following my father, who once was a uniformed security officer at the Presque Isle Air Force Base, I became a patrol boy (crossing guard) in the 7th grade, complete with a white patrol belt and badge. Wendell Monson, in the 8th grade, was my superior. The next year, I was top dog and Ronnie Sprague was my junior. I think both of those guys later became chiefs of the Fort Fairfield Police Department. I went on to work with ATF and IRS enforcement officers, sky marshals, and U.S. Attorneys.

Bloomers

Meanwhile, my sisters were busy with their own adventures. In one incident, Alana somehow stained her undies and was worried about Mom finding out. The girls tried to scrub them out but it didn't work. They decided to bury them on the Indian trail, which extended beyond the fire station past the back of our rental over the Hersey garage. They all laugh now about how Barb held that over Lanie for years, threatening to tell Mom if she didn't get her way. I don't know whether the underwear in those days had lasting, synthetic fibers, but I often envision people discovering them someday, certain they've found an Indian artifact.

Art Continues

Back at the Fort in seventh grade, I moved on to drawing imaginary car designs, historic figures, movie stars, and attractive local girls. Among my favorite subjects were Abraham Lincoln, Elvis Presley, and James Dean. I earned spending money painting dragons, tigers, eagles, horses, snakes, and more on my friends' leather jackets, even earning a winter coat by winning a Halloween poster contest.

When I was in grammar school, Ted Gagnon, head of the Chamber of Commerce and father of my longtime friend Tommy, asked me to repaint the town's eight welcome signs, which Uncle Wendell had painted years before. They read, "Welcome to Friendly Fort Fairfield, world's largest potato-producing town" (and may have noted the town's population of around six thousand). As I recall, they each consisted of four horizontal boards 1 foot by 6 feet by 2 inches, hanging by chains. Dad and I would take one sign down, put it in the trunk, bring it home, carry it up through his bedroom window, and place it on the flat roof of Hersey Chevrolet on Main Street, where I would paint them. I had agreed to do all eight signs for $30, my spending money for

the upcoming Presque Isle Fair. It took me all month, so when I finished I asked for $35. Mr. Gagnon reluctantly agreed.

When I went into high school that fall, I did the yearbook graphics and continued to draw and paint my heroes before moving on to Belfast in the spring.

Basketball

Basketball was king in Aroostook County during winter. The high-school ball players were heroes to young and old alike, as their games were broadcast on WAGM radio with the inimitable Dewey DeWitt doing the play-by-play.

We young guys all played basketball out in the snow all winter, regardless of our success at tryouts and team scrimmages inside the old high school or the new armory. If we couldn't play in or attend games, we could follow them on radio.

When I was too young to play, I had my early favorites, Larry and Keith Mahaney, who went on to more fame at the University of Maine, with Larry later becoming head of Webber Oil in Maine and a great contributor to the University. About 24 years ago, I had the great pleasure of meeting Keith again at a pancake breakfast at the old B & A Railroad Station at the Fort. He was sitting with Locky Gardner, my old grammar school principal. I remember many other great ball handlers that I admired so much: Bobby Wyman, Pete Gillespie, Bobby McDougal, Billy Mortensen, Floyd Hoyt, and my old buddy, Freddie Glew.

One of the truly amazing ballplayers of that time in the late fifties was Pete Kelley of Caribou. He was a really big guy who could make amazing turning jump shots from the corners, beyond the foul line—what is now a three-pointer. There was no way to defend against him. He is now a successful lawyer in Caribou.

One particular game, involving Bobby Wyman, stands out above all others. Bobby was a senior, captain of the team, and the principal's son. It was at the end of a tournament game in which the Fort Tigers opened against the first-place team and were a point down with just seconds to go. What Bobby did was an amazing thing, but what he said afterward was so typical of a County boy.

With the play clock ticking down to zero, Bobby heaved the ball from center court. Not only did it go in, it was a swisher and it won the game. Bobby was interviewed afterward for the radio audience. "Bobby, when you let that ball go, did you have any idea that it would go in?"

"No, but she went," was his reply.

Picking Potatoes

I've never decided which was worse, picking potatoes, picking beans, picking rocks, or raking blueberries. I've done them all, and they are back-breaking work.

Picking potatoes gets you up on a cold, fall morning, sometimes when there are clods of frost in the earth, clumping the potatoes together with dirt and rocks—not good. Even on a good day, you are bent over or on your knees, filling your basket and dumping it in a barrel, over and over, trying to keep up your section against the relentless digger, which just keeps going up and down, laying the rows bare two at a time. It's often too cold in the morning and too hot by midday, your only hope of relief being a broken digger lag or some other problem with the machinery, or a really bad rainfall. Good pickers could often fill 60 to 70 barrels in

Karen Emery in potato field

Picking rocks wasn't so bad. That had to be done in the spring to remove rocks pushed to the surface by winter frost, so that the fields could be ready for plowing, harrowing, and planting, without breaking the equipment. It involved following along a flatbed truck or wagon and tossing on the stones, some of which could be big and heavy.

Raking blueberries was done in August, usually along the rocky coast, where glacial stones and thin soil made the fields good for little else. It involved using a blueberry rake, sort of a big dustpan with tines on the front part of the bottom and a handle jutting forward over it, instead of back behind it. You could scoop the low-growing blueberries off the small plants along the ground or taller bushes by pulling the plants through the tines, leaving just the berries in the rake. Then you would dump them into bushel baskets, and turn them in when full. It was also hard on the back, unless you raked on your knees, which became a sticky affair after a while. Most rakers hated the large blueberry tarantulas that showed up on occasion, but I wasn't too bothered about them.

a day. The ultimate goal was 100 barrels in one day, but all the conditions had to be right: a good crop, big potatoes, a long day, a good-sized section you could handle, and no delays. I made it once, and I slept really well that night.

Picking beans might be better, in that the weather was warm and you could work at your own pace, not that of a digger, but you were bent over all day in the heat, and you couldn't make much money.

Saturday Night

Saturday night was a big deal in 1940s and '50s Fort Fairfield, especially during the three weeks or more of "digging" in the fall, when school would be out so the students could help harvest the potatoes.

Everybody got paid on Saturday, so we all had money to spend and shopping to do on Saturday night. It was also a time to socialize and catch up with friends and family, especially those from out of town. When we lived on lower Main Street, up over Hersey Chevrolet, Dad would park the car uptown in the afternoon to get a good spot, close to the "five and ten," in the middle of town. After a supper of baked beans, rolls, maybe sauerkraut or tripe, and coffee, we would walk up to the car and use it as our meeting point.

Kids and adults changed occupancy in the cars all evening, as cousins, uncles and aunts, and friends stopped by to chat. The parked cars were home base between short trips for groceries, new clothes, supplies, and treats. Meanwhile, the passing parade was like today's television entertainment, as nearly everyone was out, for all to see, including a harvest influx of French Canadians and Native Americans. I liked to tramp up and down the street with Uncle Bud, cousin Wayne, or cousin Fred Clark, who drove his dad's pickup over from Canada. We often liked to finish the evening with some hot French fries and a Coke.

By 1955 or '56, after the stores closed, I would often go to the apartment of newlyweds Phyllis (Chambers) and Raymond Clark, Fred's older brother, who had settled in at the end of the bridge. They were a cool young couple with the latest 45-rpm rock & roll records.

Regrettably, all of that changed after the '50s, with a switch to stores being open Friday nights, closure of the movie theater, parking meters installed for a time, and the shrinking of the Maine potato industry. Until then it had been a heady time.

1955

1955 has always been an important milestone in my mind—the difference between the past and modern times. Everything changed that year.

All the new cars had come out with hooded lights and fins, like sabre jets. The day they were unveiled, I went to the dealerships all over town to identify them

1955 Chevy

with cousin Wayne (El, as I took to calling him, because of his sideburns and ducktail). Uncle Harry bought a classic turquoise-and-cream Chevrolet from the Hersey dealership right under our apartment.

I turned 13 that year, and rock & roll came into its own, with Bill Haley and the Comets, Elvis Presley, and Little Richard. James Dean exploded on the scene and was gone. The trendy colors were pink and gray. It was an exciting time to be entering your teens. It was going to be all records and girls from now on.

We just knew America was never going to be the same, and it never was.

Mr. Cool

As a freshman in the fall of '56, I tried to be cool like cousin Wayne. I bought from Ayoob's clothing store a pair of gray dress pants and a black turtleneck, which I wore under a pink shirt with a turned-up collar and open sleeves folded up twice, with brand new white bucks like Wayne's. On the way to my first sock hop in the old high school gym, I tried to jump the little ditch down behind Jenkins Garage, didn't make it, and stained my new shoes with oil, probably dumped there by the garage. There is no way to get that off or cover it. It didn't matter too much that night because it was a sock hop. At the dance, I joined the boys on one side of the gym, while the girls stayed on the other side or danced with one another. Near the end of the evening, I finally worked up enough courage to ask an older beauty, Evie Acorn, to dance. She politely declined. Ouch. I was sorry to read recently that she had passed away.

Boob Miller

Fort Fairfield has always had its share of town characters, not just during the potato harvest and not just those related to me.

One interesting guy was Boob Miller. He lived next door to Arthur and Inez at the corner of Columbia and Milk streets. He was a very heavy man, several hundred pounds, and we used to watch his little car, a Nash Rambler, I think, groan and sink low on the driver's side whenever he got in. He was a decent, hardworking man, as far as I know.

To look at him, you might not guess that he had a reputation for being very, very strong, as did a number of men in that rugged territory, including Karen's great uncles, —Abner and Otis Ames.

In Boob's case, it was said that he could lift a full barrel of potatoes, 165 pounds, with each hand, simply by grappling onto the edge of the rim. That would take tremendous strength in the thumb and fingers, as well as the wrist and arm. I never saw him do it or heard of anyone else who would even try it.

Hattie

There were several families on the Sam Everett Road with a lot of kids. One mother complained that she did her best to keep track of hers but somehow they got by her.

"God, an elephant could get by her," Papa once quipped.

One day, one of her little girls fell out the upstairs window. The frantic mother ran out onto the lawn, picked up her unconscious daughter and berated her.

"Hattie, you cussed fool, if you're dead, I'll kill ya!"

The girl recovered.

Moxie Popham

Moxie was a large man with a stutter and seemingly the mind of a child. He went all around town by himself and everyone knew him and looked out for him. He even had his own seat at the movie hall. That's the great thing about small towns. No matter what was going on in town, Moxie would show up. He got the name Moxie when the truck driver of the famous Maine soft drink gave him a captain's cap with that logo, and Moxie was never without it from then on.

One of Uncle Harry's best stories was about Moxie. On slow days at the feed mill, Harry had lots of time to collect, embellish, and make up stories. He swore this one was true.

One night around 2 a.m. and about two miles from town, Harry was helping his neighbor's cow deliver a calf. They were suddenly startled to look up and see Moxie standing there, so they asked him to help.

"Give us a hand here, Moxie," Harry said. "We could use some help."

"N-n-n-nope," he said.

"Come on," Harry pleaded again, "reach in, grab a hold of him and pull."

Moxie was adamant, "Oha, oha, son of whore got in there by himself, I-l-let him get out by himself."

Horseshoe

I suspect that Harry appropriated the following Moxie story from another source and embellished it. It seems that Moxie wandered into Pat McKinnon's blacksmith and machine shop one morning just as Pat threw down a red-hot horseshoe. Moxie grabbed it right away and immediately flung it across the shop. The men standing around all laughed and one said, "What's the matter, Moxie, hot?"

"N-n-n-no," he said, "j-j-just don't take me long to look at a horseshoe, that's all."

Who Knew?

Finally, there was the time that the Doughty boys entrusted Moxie to drive the truck slowly up and down a field for a bunch of rock pickers. I was surprised he could drive, but they warned him not to try to go to town or even go out on the road. They then went about their other chores and left the crew on their own.

As soon as Moxie got to the bottom of the field the first time, he swung out onto the road and headed for town. He was gone several hours, but sure enough, he came back. When he pulled back into the field and stopped, the boys were all over him. "Moxie, I thought we told you not to take that truck to town," they said.

"Oha, oha, didn't know I had it," he replied.

Pick Chambers

Arnold "Pick" Chambers grew up along with the other Chambers boys, Danny, Johnny, and Jimmy, on the Sam Everett Road, about five miles out of the Fort.

The Chambers family had been there for some time, like the Doughtys, and they all went to the one-room Chambersville School. Pick lived on the edge, like so many people up there, in a little shack on the way to town. My Uncle Walter remained especially close to Pick and was always dragging him around or helping him out with one problem or another. I think he liked the fact that Pick got into a lot of minor scrapes that made for good stories to pass around.

I don't know how he got the nickname "Pickaxe," but it may have had to do with the fact that he was small and thin, the size of an axe handle, and had a beaked nose. The Doughty boys used to say, "Pick was so thin he had to stand sideways so you could see him."

He had a boy who looked just like him.

Sam Bentley

I first remember Sam when, as a fairly old man, he would ride all over town on an old bicycle, including out to Cheney Grove, to pick up knives, scissors, and other things that needed sharpening. He must have done a good job, as I was given one of his saws about 40 years ago and I haven't had to sharpen it to this day.

Sam's past was not exactly clear to everyone, but it was rumored that he was part Indian and may have killed a man with his bare hands in his youth. I got to see more of him in the 1950s, when he lived in a little log cabin next to my Uncle Earle and Aunt Madeline Hansen, down behind the Episcopal Church on the riverbank. Both places were flooded up to the ceiling during the ice-out of the Aroostook River in 1952.

Madeline befriended Sam and often did little things for him. As a result, Sam often became a pest, clumping in with his cane two or three times a day, gumming tobacco or Red Top with no teeth and spitting out the juice. She was especially annoyed in the wintertime when he punctured her linoleum with his creepers or ice cleats.

Two or three times a year, Sam would be visited for

a few weeks by his friend Frank Pelky. They would eat beans and molasses, drink, talk loudly, and sometimes go on a toot or get into a squabble. Frank would stay until they couldn't stand one another any longer, then he would leave. He always said, "I make people happy twice when I visit—happy to see me come and happy to see me go."

Of his friend Sam, Frank used to say, "Here comes ol' Satan with his stinger hanging out (tongue wagging). Sam is so cantankerous that, when he dies, they're going to bury him pizzle end up, so when he tries to dig himself out, he'll only go deeper."

Border Security

In the mid 1900s, border security was more relaxed, as evidenced by the Doughty's private road through the woods from their farm into Canada.

Yet, even then, you easily could get into trouble. One time I drove up to the boundary line at the Fort to impress my kids and their cousins with how easily we could cross into another country. After pointing out the two international guard stations, I pulled up into the school-bus turnaround and, without realizing it, crossed the border illegally. All kinds of bells and sirens went off as the agents quickly intercepted us. The kids were all very impressed that day, as "Uncle Dave almost got arrested."

The border patrol on both sides was very friendly with the locals and usually was very aware of what was going on in the border communities. When I stopped in recent years at the Canadian checkpoint with a car full of relatives heading for Aunt Helen's funeral, the guard asked, "Going to the Clark service?"

A few years before, I stopped at the American side upon reentry with another car full of relatives. The guard on duty had served there many years and was known for his habit of asking all where they were born. This time my aunt (I won't say which one) answered, "You know where I was born, you damned fool."

Local Expressions

Before I leave the County, I want to go over some common expressions, just to give you a flavor of how different things were from where you might be.

Bud's Own

Uncle Bud had his own expressions, most of them nonsensical and for his own amusement, but not all of them.

Hoppose, *skiddaballs*, and *squeegee for a mograb* were all just nonsensical things he made up, as far as I know.

Hipoppopalus was some kind of unknown illness, like "the scol' paunch."

The Wee Diddidaro was what he called my infant cousin, Glenda Clark.

Doodiddidaw was Bud's word for doohicky, thingamajig, wachamacallit, thingy.

She is but she ain't, she ain't but she is. I don't know where Bud got that or what he meant by it, but it does nicely describe the complexities of a woman.

Don't take any wooden nickels was a favorite expression others also used.

It's good for what ails you is the way Bud and others described food and drink.

Can't afford it was Bud's answer to anything he didn't want to do.

"Li'l Liza Jane" was one of Bud's favorite old fiddle tunes. It also happened to be Great Grandmother Estey's name. Bud picked up and often sang some very funny and slightly off-color words to the song, but I won't repeat them here. Some in the family will remember them.

Hi dee hey, hi dee ho, listen to the radio, pahdaw, pahdah, pahdaw, pahdaw. I suspect Bud somehow appropriated this from Cab Calloway and made it his own.

Raise hell and *shit in the brook* would be a rebellious thing to do, indeed, if others got their drinking water from it, as did the Doughtys. In fact, the outhouse on the farm was strategically placed downstream of the farmhouse.

Awwwbverrreech may have been Bud's strangest and most entertaining expression of all. It was usually accompanied by grabbing his or (better still) someone else's shirtsleeve between his thumb and forefinger and shaking vigorously. Others would be quizzical, if not astonished by this, but his young nieces and nephews would break out into gales of laughter, and still do at the very mention of it.

County Sayings

Whoop and drive 'er really represents the County to me. It was a very common expression. It probably originated from driving horses, but it came to mean face the task square on and push through it, without hesitation. In today's lexicon it might be "Let 'er rip," "Go for it," "Get 'er done," or "Just do it." It was a common attitude and work ethic in my family and the English-Irish-Scot community at large. Its later use probably developed from the tough climate, poor economic conditions, and hard work necessary just to survive.

Are you workin'? This was one of the most common greetings in the County. If you were, you and your family were probably all right. The last thing anybody wanted was to be "on the town," although, a lot of people had to be, from time to time. To be working often meant that you were able and willing to do a lot of different things in order to put food on the table. Thus, there were a lot of jacks-of-all-trades, like my father, and very

few specialists. It also meant that people could do for themselves quite nicely, maybe with a little help from friends and family, but without hiring outsiders.

Chimbley meant chimney.

Christer was a badly behaving child, as in "a regular little Christer." Go figure.

Crazier than a shithouse rat speaks for itself.

Culch was nothing but trash, junk, or bad stuff.

Dooryard was the front yard or front driveway.

Don't make me come back there or *If I have to stop this car and come back there, you're going to be some sorry, mister man.* Clear enough.

Gallivant or *traipse* meant flit about.

Gawm meant a klutz or to grab (onto) clumsily. *Gawmy* meant clumsy.

Gorby referred to a glutton. It's a gray jay that often stole woodsmen's sandwiches.

Hump meant move right along, as in "He was really humpin' it.

I'll slap you silly was another threat to kids.

I scream, you scream, we all scream for ice scream was popular everywhere.

Jeezer meant chap or fellow, maybe hellion, as in "tough little jeezer."

Jeezly meant goddamned or cursed, as in "I couldn't get the top off the jeezly thing."

Jillpoke meant a slow, useless worker, as in "He was nothin' but a jillpoke."

Larrupin' meant moving fast or a beating or "lickin."

Looks like something the cat drug in: not a good look, as you can imagine.

Muckle or grab onto that.

Number'n a pounded thumb meant stupid

Ptetters or *spuds* are potatoes.

Puckerbrush: tangled bushes that were hard to get through.

Rumdum: drunkard.

Son of a whore sounds bad but it rolled nicely off the tongue of those who cursed regularly. It was often a term of endearment, as in, "How are you, you old son of a whore?" It could also mean damned thing, as in "I worked on the car all day but I couldn't get the son of a whore to start."

Spittin' image means looks just like, as in "He's the spittin' image of his dad.

Spleeny meant one who doesn't deal well with pain.

Stave up meant to tear up, mess up, or destroy, as in, "He was all stove up."

Three sheets to the wind meant drunk.

Tunk was a light blow, as in "I gave him a tunk up 'side the head.

Two piss holes in the snow: the way the eyes look after a night of drinking.

Walk it right to her Meant don't hold back, work hard at it.

Walk right back on 'er was to pull hard, carry your weight, or give it your all.

Whistle referred to the throat, as in, "I'm going to wet my whistle."

Wreck of the Hesperus was a look worse than a bad hair day.

Yank you bald-headed was a threat to misbehaving kids.

Yes, now I betcha was a way to say "I knew this was going to happen."

Yow-uns meant young ones or kids.

An Aroostook Vignette

The following is made up, just to give you a flavor of how these expressions might be used in everyday life. Probably most people in Aroostook don't curse like this, and those who do are not necessarily being disparaging or disrespectful. It's often just the way they talk.

Perley had been gallivanting all over creation. Now here he come, just a larrupin', really humpin' it, hauling into the dooryard to a screeching stop. He was about three sheets to the wind, his eyes like two piss holes in the snow. He was the spittin' image of his dad, who was a bit of a rumdum, but right now, Perley looked like something the cat drug in. He was number than a pounded thumb, but he was a good guy.

"How are you, you old son of a whore?" Bumpy asked. "Muckle onto this barrel of pteters and walk right back on 'er." Perley gawmed onto it like a gorby, Bumpy hollered "Whoop and drive 'er," and they hoisted it onto the truck bed.

In the process, Perley tore his glove and cut his hand. He wasn't spleeny, so all he said was, "Yes, now I'll betcha. Them gloves are brand new too." He simply took them off and scaled them into the puckerbrush. That give him a catch in the hoozler, he said, as he took out his bottle of culch to wet his whistle before leaving to check on the yow-uns. Just then he dropped his bottle and it shattered in the gravel. "Now wouldn't that make a dog's ass want to suck a lemon," he exclaimed.

Wasting even bad booze made Perley crazier than a shithouse rat.

"Well, I can't stand around here all day like a jeezly jillpoke," he said. With that, he jumped back into his stove-up Desoto, really walked it to 'er, and was gone out of sight in no time flat.

Coastal Lingo

After we moved to the coast, we found that region had its own set of expressions.

Ayuh (yeah, yes) is everyone's idea of Downeast talk.

De-ah (dear) is a term of endearment or just a way of addressing man or woman.

Daow is an emphatic no or no way.

Godfrey is a polite word for God, so as not to curse.

Gorry or *gorry be* means golly.

Gorry sakes alive! Well, for God's sake!

Bugs, spidahs are common terms for lobstah.

Some implies quite or very special, as in "That's some horse you have there."

Wa'nt means wasn't or weren't, as in "I tried it but it wa'nt too good."

Wicked means extremely, as in "It was wicked (or awful) good."

There are a lot more sayings well described in other books about Maine, but this should give you a good idea of the language differences between the County and the coast, differences that are becoming less prominent.

Belfast

When we moved to Belfast in 1957, it had about 6,500 people, like Fort Fairfield, but was a very different place. Fort has only about 3,000 now. The population of Belfast has remained about the same for 100 years.

Far from acres of potato fields, Belfast had the harbor; clamming, fishing, and lobstering; factories and wonderful captains' mansions with widow walks; and two poultry plants that gave the place an odorous rap at low tide. We had come from the potato capital of the world to the broiler capital. Patti Page was out with her big hit "Old Cape Cod" that year, and that's the way I felt about Belfast. I just felt we were on the other side of the Haynesville woods and into civilization.

The movie *Peyton Place* was filmed here and in nearby Camden that year, and many people said that's the way Belfast really was. "If you want to go to hell fast, go to Belfast" was a common refrain. One story circulating was about the girl who went to the doctor, learned that she was pregnant, and insisted over and over that she hadn't done anything. Finally, the doctor relented, "It's that goddamned Belfast water!" We loved it here, and the water was fine.

One of the other big differences from Aroostook that gave us endless entertainment was the funny way people talked, with a Downeast, rather than a Canadian, accent. "Cah" instead of "car." "Bayah" instead of "bear." "Lobstah" instead of "lobster." We used to laugh every night about what we had heard. One of our favorite records was "Bert and I" by Maine humorists Robert Bryan and Marshall Dodge.

I had a terrific school career at Crosby High School, starting with my sophomore year. I made a number of lifelong friends, including Doug and Gail (Snow) Smith, Gary and Roberta (Robbins) Walker, John "Pat" and Brenda (Sproul) Mullen, John Rohde, and very special friend, Joanne Boynton, all of whom are back in town and seen quite often. I was lucky to be very popular in school and into a lot of activities, including sports,

Crosby Lion decal, 1959

Lincoln, 1958 (age 16), household enamel, 13" X 9"

plays, debating, and student government. I drew and painted real and imaginary characters, designed and illustrated yearbooks, created the school logo, and "flamed" friends' cars. When I finished high school at the top of my class, I had accumulated many boxes of realistic drawings and paintings. Norman Rockwell's Famous Artist School tried to recruit me, but my guidance counselor, Larry Lewis, steered me toward the Rhode Island School of Design. He even arranged for me to travel there with Fran Merritt, director of Haystack Mountain School of Crafts, now on Deer Isle.

Karen and I moved back to Belfast in 2002. What a great place it is now. The poultry plants are long gone, replaced by MBNA (now Bank of America), Athena Health, and now Front Street Shipyard, as the largest employers. The city is full of art galleries, upscale stores and restaurants, many other creative businesses, and natives mixing with artists, writers, performers, and newcomers from away. The place is often written up in magazines as the up-and-coming place to be.

There is no place else we'd rather be. That just happens to be the theme of the 2010 AARP calendar, featuring my 2006 painting *Belfast Summer Nights*, an image of my father at a summer concert in the harbor the year before he died.

Bandstand

That first year in Belfast, I was very taken with the girl next door. Ellen Hopkins was two years younger than me but she was very attractive and mature for her age. My sister Barbara and I, plus Ellen and her brothers, Barry and Steve, along with Roberta Thompson (the neighbor on the other side of our house) and her friend, Patty Black, all used to gather at Ellen's every afternoon after boys' basketball practice to watch Dick Clark's *American Bandstand* on TV. Her mother, Dot, loved Coca Cola and was like a kid herself. She and her husband, Al, who was a meat cutter at the A & P, were happy to have the kids all there where they could keep an eye on them. Some 25 years later in New Jersey, I had neighbors from south Philly who knew Bob, Justine, and many other *Bandstand* regulars.

Belfast Summer Nights, 2006 oil, 16" X 24"

The Nose

My father had a prominent "Roman" nose, which he clearly got from his father. I don't know how far back it goes, but it is a family trait that has left its mark, to a greater or lesser degree, on succeeding generations. I think it was what Dad and his sisters were thinking of in the following story.

In her late years, Gram was bragging over and over about what a beautiful and smart little boy Dad had been, with his (then) blond hair and ability to go to the nearby store and bring back the correct change, and so forth. One of his sisters, Alda, listened to all this for a while and then she said, "Gee, Ran, what happened?"

Not to be outdone, Dad immediately came back with an explanation. "Well, as I got older, I began to look more like my sisters."

Dad's prominent proboscis loomed large in an incident one night over 50 years ago, during supper in Belfast. My sister Cheryl was late getting home and we had started supper without her. Everyone knew Dad insisted we not be late for supper.

Suddenly, Cheryl opened the kitchen door right up against Dad's chair. When she did, the legs went out from under him, and he was sitting flat on the floor, with his nose resting right on the edge of the table. Everyone was in shock, waiting to see what would happen next.

"Where the hell have you been?" he asked.

"Only the nose knows," she said. "Speak, beak!"

We thought he was going to kill her, but suddenly, everyone, including Dad, broke out into uncontrollable laughter. I don't know where she came up with that, but she clearly dodged a bullet that night.

Stowaway

Years later, Cheryl and her husband, Ken Gilmore, had a neighbor in Corinna who drove a Greyhound bus. He used to give the local kids a ride on weekends but he was apparently a stickler for rules on the job.

One day an old lady tried to board with her small dog, but the driver explained that he couldn't allow the dog on the bus. She protested that the dog would be no trouble and could sit on her lap, all to no avail. Finally, in frustration, she said, "Well, you know what you can do with this bus don't you?"

"Yup, and if you can do the same thing with the dog, you can get on," he answered.

Bill Knight

One of Dad's Belfast cronies was Bill Knight. Bill ran a heating and appliance business in his own, inimitable way.

One time Dad went with him on a sales visit to Swanville. The woman wanted a new electric stove, but Bill wanted to sell her a gas stove, which heated more quickly and for which he could continue to sell her bottled gas. She wasn't convinced.

"I'm afraid of gas," she said. "Besides, I don't think it's that much quicker."

"I tell you what," he said. "We'll both strip down, I'll sit my bare ass on the electric stove, you sit yours on the gas stove, we'll turn 'em on and see who moves first."

"SOLD!" she exclaimed.

Harry Snow

Harry Snow was janitor at the First National Bank of Belfast, now Key Bank, and I became his assistant after school and on weekends. Harold Stone was the bank president then and Claude Clements, the vice president.

Harry was a great guy with a calm demeanor and a dry sense of humor. We had a routine during the week of lowering the flag on top of the building, dusting, emptying the ashtrays, filling the coal hopper, sweeping and buffing the floors, and so on. On Saturdays, we were up early, raising the flag, polishing the brass plates outside, checking the furnace, bringing the money trays out of the vault, and generally preparing for the opening. We always took time about 7 a.m. to get fresh donuts from Weaver's Bakery down the street to go with our fresh coffee from the kitchen. The rest of the morning, we cleaned the law offices of Eaton & Glass, which were in the building. Saturday afternoons were like the others, except we washed and buffed the floors and sometimes washed the windows in the bank and the law offices. One time, as we were working hard to get the flyspecks off the big windows, Harry remarked,

"There never was and never will be a constipated fly."

One Saturday afternoon, early on, I dropped an empty metal pail going down the concrete and metal stairs to the basement, right behind Harry. It made a hell of a noise in the big, empty building. Harry didn't even flinch or react at all, except to say quietly, "Something's on the drop."

As we were outside polishing the brass one morning, one of Harry's childhood friends stopped to chat. Apparently, he had always been much more interested in playing the horses than holding down a steady job like Harry's. That day, he chided his old school chum. "Harry," he said, "do you realize your life is nothing but a battle with dirt?"

Harry had blueberries out in Liberty, so during the two weeks of that harvest in August, he was out there and I was head janitor. Each morning, after I got the bank ready, I loaded the back of his pickup with young rakers and drove them out to the field, then I picked them up at the end of the day and brought them back, usually after a delivery of the day's harvest to the nearby Monmouth cannery. If I transported kids in an open pickup today, I would be stopped by police and charged with endangerment.

Harry and his wife, Flossie, had been high school sweethearts. She was now disabled and used a wheelchair. They had a collection of *National Geographic* magazines going back to 1921, which they gave me. It was a treasure trove of fascinating stories, pictures, advertising, and illustrations by some of America's greatest artists.

Mr. Dithers

I don't remember his real name, but he looked like Dagwood Bumstead's boss in the comic strip *Blondie*, so the class called him that.

He was substituting for "Bulldog" Green, our physics teacher at Crosby High. This particular day, Mr. Dithers was explaining the concept of inertia and momentum, the idea that big things are hard to move but, once they are moving, are hard to stop. He told about his son piloting a tug he was not familiar with and how he couldn't slow it down fast enough coming into port. Then the story stopped and Mr. Dithers started on his next teaching point. We all stopped him and asked what had happened with the tug.

"Well," he said, in true Yankee fashion, "he crashed that dock somethin' fierce."

SATs

A bunch of us were making our way on snowy roads from Belfast to the University of Maine to take our Scholastic Aptitude Tests (SATs).

Elsie Boynton, our beloved English teacher and advisor, let me drive her green '57 Chevy wagon, carrying her, her daughter Joanne and her younger daughter, Sally. As we reached a long hill in Stockton Springs, Terry Porter and his girlfriend, Joline Kenny, went by us in his father's Volkswagen beetle and on out of sight over the hill. When I topped the crest, I saw their car down over a bank and upside down, with no movement around it. I stopped our car and ran down to see if they were all right, just as Joline, still upside down, was rolling down the window.

"I looked out, saw nothing but white, and thought we had died and gone to heaven," she said. They were okay, but we were all a little shaken. Regardless, we went on to Orono and took our SATs after calling Dr. Porter to come get the car. I think we all did pretty well on the test too.

RISD

After graduating from high school in 1960, I went to the Rhode Island School of Design. It has made all the difference in my life. I felt like I was born again, starting school all over, getting my first real art training. I went there secretly wanting to be Norman Rockwell, the famous illustrator for the *Saturday Evening Post,* but the plan was to go into industrial design and combine my artistic and engineering promise. By the end of freshman year, I went into illustration. I was at the top of the class by the end of sophomore year, but longed to join those creative fine-art painters. My painting instructor and advisor, Robert Hamilton, cautioned that, in so doing, I might forfeit my certain chance of going to Italy my senior year, wouldn't be able to make a living at painting, and wouldn't be

Seated Female Nude, RISD, 1962 charcoal, 28" x 20"

able to support a family unless I became a teacher. I switched anyway, with his blessing, and still went to Italy, with him as the onsite coordinator.

At RISD, arguably the best art school in the country, I immersed myself in the creative process, the history of art, and the study of creative giants like Pablo Picasso and Willem de Kooning, who are still major influences on my work. The conceptual thinking, ability to solve problems, and design integrity that I learned there also served me well throughout a public affairs career in government. RISD greatly enhanced the way I appreciate art and life.

Summer of '63

It was a magical time. I was home from RISD for the summer, before going to Italy. I rented a studio space above what is now the Parent Gallery and a gallery space in what is now the High Street Market, each for $20 a month. The latter was across the street from Dad's 2nd floor office, where he served as the "county agent," and from Carbone's gift store, where he worked weekends and where Bella Books is now located. The

Route 1 summer traffic went right through town on High Street then, and I made my biggest sale to that point when a New York couple bought a large semi-abstract figure drawing for $500 and drove off with it in the back of their sports convertible. I also was commissioned by my former English teacher and dear friend, Elsie Boynton, to paint her beautiful 10-year-old daughter, Sally (now married to Tom Savage). At the end of the summer, I also painted the portrait of a young widow in Bayside, whose name escapes me.

That summer, my sister Barbara married Paul Vosburgh after a tumultuous courtship. I was permitted to join their gang of friends, consisting of Jerry Savitz (now owner of Darby's Restaurant), Johnny Jenks, Virgil Fowles, Anita Ward, and several others. Almost every night, after work, they met on a beach somewhere, built a fire, steamed clams, and drank cold beer, iced down in the trunk of Jerry's car. I also enjoyed getting to know budding poet Eugene Mahoney, known to us as "Dumas," and getting close to the beautiful Paula (Clark) Manning. At the end of summer, I left for Rome.

Italy

In 1963-64, I spent my senior year with RISD studying painting in Rome as part of the European Honors Program. I went over on the Italian cruise ship *Michelangelo* and went through a three-day hurricane on the way. It was the start of many adventures that year.

I lived with a poor Italian family that didn't speak English. They treated me like a son. Their youngest, eight-year-old Maurizio, was like my shadow. For Christmas, they gave me a 45-rpm record of a new English group, the Beatles, with "Please Please Me" on one side and "I Want to Hold Your Hand" on the other. Shortly thereafter, I befriended a British soldier on leave who told of another band that was going to be even bigger, called the Rolling Stones. When Karen and I went back to Rome for a RISD reunion 31 years later, we found Maurizio, who was now 40 and looked just like his father had.

In the fall of '63 our group of 19 RISD students visited the great art treasures of Italy the first several weeks, then we settled in Rome. We went to the tops of Mount Vesuvius and the Leaning Tower of Pisa, saw the ruins of Pompeii and the depths of the catacombs, enjoyed the canals of Venice and the splendors of Florence, and had an audience with Pope Paul VI. I later drove to Paris for two weeks with fellow student Hiroshi Murata in his Austin Healy Sprite. The mountain passes were closed, so we went under the Alps to France in a pitch-black train tunnel, riding in the vehicle on a flatcar throughout the night.

In Paris we went to the Louvre museum; the Modern Museum; the Jeu de Paume Museum of impressionist works, where the Nazis once hid their stolen art; Notre Dame Cathedral; and the Crazy Horse Salon. Mostly we hung out with his Japanese friend Shoro Kawazoe, who was studying flamenco guitar and years later brought the musical *Hair* to Japan. His stepfather was a well-known cellist, Gaspar Cassado. At night we watched Sho and his Spanish friends perform flamenco and drank with his artist friends in a cold Montmartre walkup. Paris and Rome were unbelievably exciting, with all of the great art, beautiful women, savory food, fascinating culture, and ancient history. I also found the Italians far more affectionate and outgoing than my Irish Catholic family back in Maine.

I convinced our oversight professor, Robert Hamilton, who many years later became a well-known

David in Rome, 1963 (Photo by Joan Kokkins Herron)

painter and good friend back in Maine, to let me have the unheated attic of Palazzo Cenci as my studio. It was indeed cool, with a paving stone floor and huge support rafters. I was thrilled to learn later that David Macaulay, author of *How Things Work*, followed me into that studio and illustrated it in his book *Rome Antics.* By 1995, RISD had developed the space into three studios.

Over the winter, Hiroshi accidentally cut the tendon in his left wrist and was unable to drive his car back across Rome from a repair shop. He asked me to go with him and shift. So I sat on his left and shifted while he sat on the right in the British car and drove through rush-hour traffic and around the monument circles across the city. It was a gutsy thing to do, especially since Italians drove like madmen, but we were young and foolish enough to try and succeed.

I went to the New Year's party at the American Academy in Rome dressed as a bare-chested pirate in clothes I got at the flea market. An Italian filmmaker offered me a part in a movie he was planning, but I left Italy before he got started. 35 years later in Philly, I met a lady who had been at that party and had taken my picture. In April, I left a month early and hitchhiked through Italy, Monaco, Spain, Morocco, and Gibraltar. In Algeciras, Spain, home of the great bullfighter, Manolete, I discovered a yard full of steam engines and met the brother of Cuba's ousted Batista, a big man in town who introduced me to paella. I also discovered that two girls living at his pension were from an earlier class at RISD. A year later, one of them came to Belfast to see me before riding across the country on horseback.

Two other girls, from Pembroke College, who had joined us in Italy, were murdered while hitchhiking in Germany after we left.

Army Life

When I came home from Italy in 1964, I was drafted into the army. After boot camp at Fort Dix, NJ, I ended up in an art shop at Fort Meade, MD with a few other draftees, making illustrations, silk-screen posters, and other recruiting materials during the Vietnam War. There I learned a classic lesson on how to get along in the military.

The other guys and I affectionately called the oldest and most experienced illustrator "Sarge." He was only a Spec-4, but he was in charge. One day, the door burst open and the colonel brought the post fire marshal in for a spot inspection. No one got up to stand at attention or salute, as required. They announced their purpose, and, with a cigarette dangling from his lip, Sarge said, "Okay, Sarge" to the officers. They ignored his affront and went to their work.

"What the hell is this five-gallon can of lacquer

thinner doing in here? That's highly explosive and supposed to be kept out in the shed," the fire marshal shouted.

"I don't know, Sarge; we've never had any problems," was the response.

"I guess not," the officer said, "because if you did, this whole (bleep)ing headquarters would be blown sky high." With that, they turned and abruptly left. We never heard any more. I guess they figured we were too dumb to discipline.

Two of the more interesting guys in my barracks, opposites who hung out together, were Dinges, a streetwise toughy from New York, and Hoyt Fincher from the South. Dinges teased Fincher mercilessly. One night after lights out, Dinges hollered, "Hoyt, these guys all think you're just a dumb country bumpkin, but I want to prove you're not. Go ahead, Hoyt, and name a citrus fruit."

"Leave me alone, Dinges," he hollered back, but Dinges kept it up. Finally, after about the third request, Hoyt relented and offered in a quiet voice, "A banana?"

Not long after, Hoyt announced one Saturday morning that Dinges was taking him to see the Washington Monument. That was great, we all thought,

Mock-Up of Army Poster, circa 1967, poster paint & pencil, 14" X 11"

but they were back in about a half hour. Washington was at least a half hour away, so we began to inquire.

"Oh, no," Hoyt said, "it's right around the corner, but it's a lot smaller than I thought it was." It turns out that Dinges had taken him to see a local cemetery obelisk just outside the post.

One of my good army buddies, who served with me briefly, Jim Hall, contacted me from Missouri 45 years later. He had found my website on the Internet. I had been Jim's best man at a private army wedding. In the course of catching up after all these years, he reminded me that I also had drawn his portrait. He still had it and asked whether it might be worth something now.

"Hang onto it," I advised him. "One of us could still amount to something."

Green Beret

While I was at the 2nd Army Recruiting Command, my boss, Captain Rhoda Messer, set up a press conference featuring Barry Sadler, who was passing by and had a big hit song about the Vietnam War, "Ballad of the Green Beret."

"Flighty," as the guys called her, was a little bitty thing and all a-twitter that day over her publicity coup. Things were going very well until a reporter asked Sadler, an actual Green Beret, as I recall, what he thought of women in the army.

Without hesitation, our hero said, "I love WACs: I think every soldier should be issued one."

Needless to say, the Captain was livid and highly agitated that day.

James

I was sitting at the Lighthouse bar outside Fort Meade talking to a battle-hardened marine when James stopped behind us with his wet mop.

James was a mentally-challenged kid from a local institution, who cleaned up for George Kiriazoglou, the owner. James was very big, with very dark skin, a thick neck, bullet head, and heavy brow, under which the whites of his eyes were set deep in shadow. This day, he obviously wanted us to move so he could finish mopping up, but the marine was so engrossed in his story that he was slow in noticing James's presence. Soon the marine became vaguely aware of the eyes burning holes in the back of his head. He partially turned and said, "Oh, hi, Jim," and quickly returned to his story.

James laid a huge hand on his shoulder and said in a deep voice, "How you know my name?"

As if suddenly aware of an ominous danger, the marine quickly blurted, "I don't know your name, you kiddin' me?" Then he hightailed it out of there.

Fire

Another time, James had gone out to burn the trash in a fairly strong wind. He was soon back, trying to interrupt George's story at the bar. "George, George, George," he kept repeating. George kept telling him to wait a minute.

Finally, after several minutes had gone by, George asked, "What is it, Jim?"

"Fire," James said. We all rushed out to see that the fire had gotten away from him and into the nearby grass. We ran for the hose, while James got down on his hands and knees and tried to snuff the flames with his big hands. Luckily we got it under control pretty quickly, and James seemed none the worse for wear.

Dick Nixon

I'm including here a couple of incidents because they are funny, not because they have anything to do with my connection to Aroostook. I did actually see Nixon once. I was invited to take my wife and baby boy to a ceremony at the Nixon White House for Romanian President Nicolae Ceausescu, who later was hanged by his own people during a freedom uprising. But that's another story.

I had just joined the IRS National Training Center in the early 1970s when I was assigned to do research on a film we were making with Kentucky Public Television about the history of taxation. I visited the National Archives to see what they might contribute. My contact there was a young, nerdy-looking guy who took me way up to the top floor and into a small locked room under the roof. As we were looking over labels on the file cabinets, I noticed a little handmade sign on top of one, so I went over for a closer look.

"Dick Nixon before he dicks us," it read.

I imagined this as his secret political statement, locked well away from the eyes of his superiors. Little did I realize at the time that, within a few years, my IRS office in Baltimore would be investigating Nixon and Vice President Agnew.

LBJ

I also saw LBJ and his family on the White House lawn once, but that is neither here nor there.

A few years before that and while I was in the Army at Fort Meade, I was relieving myself one night at a urinal in the Lighthouse bar, outside the post. Naturally, I was looking over graffiti written on the prophylactic dispensers on the wall in front of me, perhaps with somewhat of a blurred vision—I don't remember. I do remember that one was about the President and was particularly memorable.

"These here safes work real good." Signed LBJ.

Art Ventures

Because I can draw and paint, I've taken on some odd projects over the years.

Two summers while I was in college, I worked for Fred and Flo Bastion at the Mooring Restaurant in East Belfast, now Papa J's. I also painted boiled lobsters in house paint on two large panels on either side of the entrance. Maybe thirty years later, I saw a similar piece in Jerry Savitz's Chowder House and was informed by the young coat-check attendant that it was mine and that Jerry, who now owns Darby's Restaurant, had rescued and saved both of them. Many of my hand-printed labels for the stuffed animals at "world-famous" Perry's Nut House in Belfast enjoy a similar fate 53 years later at a local antiques store.

While in the army and just back from studying art in Italy, I painted two murals in a new bar and restaurant Jimmy Andrew was opening on Route 40 outside Baltimore. One was a number of cupids on the pink wall of Cupid's Lounge. The other was Mediterranean scenery in Dimitri's Restaurant. A year later, the place was sold and became a funeral parlor. The murals were painted over.

Once out of the army but still in the area, I painted two six-foot termites on the sides of one or more trucks for Rudd's Pest Control in Annapolis, MD. That harkens back to a poster-size fly I did for Molly Towle's science class in grammar school, which she hung over her home fireplace.

Besides teaching art on the side, I did a lot of commissioned portraits in the late '60s to help meet my new mortgage payments. One of them, while I was still in the army, was of a general, who was a family friend of an army buddy in trouble for shenanigans at the Playboy Club in Baltimore. He wanted to give it to the general in hopes that it might save him from going to Korea, which it apparently did. Since he was also an illustrator, I bet he painted his own name over mine on it. Regardless, he paid me with a $500 set of stainless steel cookware he was peddling, which I still have today.

I used the new acrylic paints to do the portraits because they dried very fast and I could knock them out quickly, sometimes working from a Polaroid picture I took on the spot. The fastest one I ever did was of a GI I had been drinking with at the Lighthouse. He asked me at the 2 a.m. closing if I could do his portrait in uniform that night as a Christmas present for his parents. He was

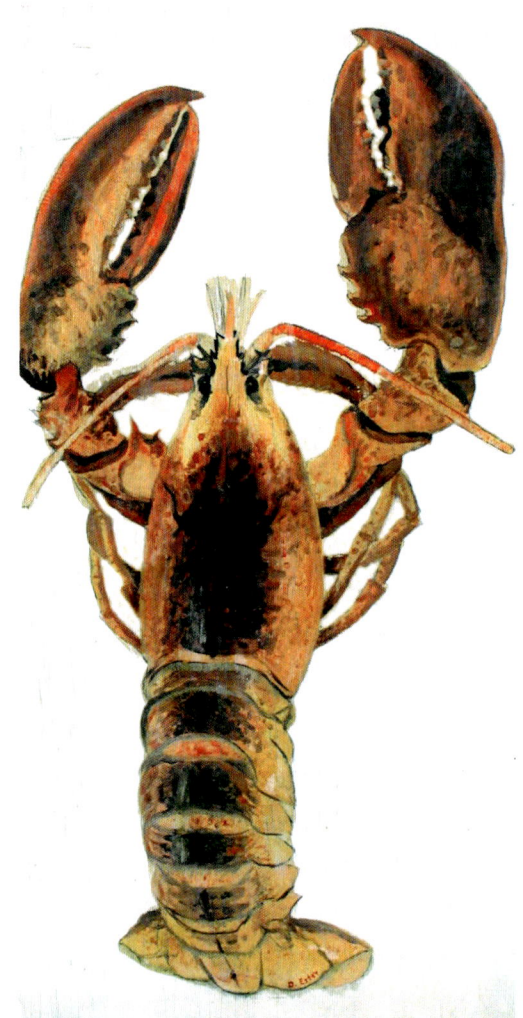

Lobster sign, 1962 household enamel, 48" X 24"

flying out later in the morning, so I snapped his picture, went home and knocked out a portrait, and met him at 7 a.m. in the Baltimore/Washington Airport with the finished piece.

IRS

By 1969, I had grown tired of illustrating for the army and was stuck in my career, so I joined Internal Revenue Service as a visual information specialist at the IRS National Training Center in Crystal City (Arlington), Virginia. It was a kind of think tank. There I illustrated pilot training programs, including some for Alcohol, Tobacco, and Firearms, focusing on bomb detection and sky marshal duties. I advanced nicely and was lined up to work for a supposed shoe-in to head up a new ATF, out from under IRS. However, my guy was overlooked when the White House named G. Gordon Liddy, later known for masterminding the Watergate break-in. Thus began my 26-year IRS career, primarily in public affairs.

David on WJZ TV-13, in Baltimore circa 1974

In 1973, I became public affairs officer for the IRS Baltimore District, which covered Maryland and D.C. and was then investigating Watergate. There I became spokesperson for many high-profile tax cases and started my own radio and TV programs, including the first nationwide tax-help program on PBS. It was a fascinating job. I produced thousands of feature articles, newsletters, news releases, policies, procedures, programs, public service announcements, responses to media inquiries, scripts, and speeches. I dealt with accountants, lawyers, Congressional staff, agency heads, and news media, including Walter Cronkite and Bob Woodward, of Watergate fame. While there, I also earned a master's degree in public administration from George Washington University.

Roots

One of my fellow managers, Julius Coleman, was a childhood friend of author Alex Haley in Frederick, MD. He said that for several years, whenever he visited the Haleys, they would say Alex was at the library researching family history. In 1979, Haley's *Roots: The Next Generation,* the story of several generations of African Americans starting from the first brought to the U.S. as a slave, was made into a powerful TV series. I was so moved by the 13 weekly episodes that I wrote an essay for the employee newsletter on the important lessons for all of us.

Heady Times

In 1974, a new district director, Gerald G. Portney, became my boss. He was perhaps the most brilliant guy I ever met in government. Many years later, I painted a tribute to him called *The Leader,* which I used as the poster image for my Philadelphia solo exhibit, *Inside the IRS.*

Jerry reopened a tax audit of President Nixon and disallowed a tax deduction for his presidential papers worth a quarter of a million dollars. He also opened a bribery investigation of Vice President Agnew, led by 30-year-old Eugene "Pete" Twardowicz, who was unique at following the money. There were many other high-profile investigations, but none of greater import. Within a year, both sides met in a motel in Alexandria, VA and agreed to a plea bargain. Agnew resigned in disgrace, pled *nolo contendere* (no contest) to one count, and avoided prison.

Pete Twardowicz became much in demand

The Leader (Gerald G. Portney), 1998 oil, 36" X 48"

at several agencies to teach his money-laundering investigative techniques. He was forced to leave his beloved Baltimore and become a manager in Washington. Years later I heard that he had became an alcoholic and died early of a heart attack.

Only in America could a 30-year-old paper pusher topple the second most powerful man in the world without someone stopping him. Others believe he wasn't stopped because everyone along the line worried about his own neck.

When I had gone home to Fort Fairfield for Christmas in 1968, before starting my job at IRS, Uncle Harry and Uncle Walter were appalled that I would be working for an outfit known in those parts for "driving up in a big Cadillac and taking farmers' farms." Walter said the whole bunch of them ought to be strung up, along with Earl Warren's Supreme Court. Harry said, "People used to visit Washington to see the cherry blossoms; now they go to see the taxpayers' skins hung up to dry."

That wasn't my experience at all. I found IRS to be the most dedicated, fair, honest, and professional government agency of all that I encountered. For years I had a 24-7 job, explaining complex tax law in simple terms, matching wits with smart, investigative reporters, and standing in the doorway as spokesperson between IRS bureaucrats and the public/media. It was an invigorating education about how and why our democracy works, and I was a proud public servant. I also got to see nine presidents and vice presidents during my career.

Susie

My first wife, Aloisia "Susie" (Eron), was from Vienna, Austria. She came to this country married to a GI who worked for NSA, the spy agency, where I happened to have had my first solo exhibit.

I met her in 1964, while in the army at Fort Meade. She worked for the Kiriazoglous, a Greek-American family, at the Three Pigs restaurant and Lighthouse bar, just outside the post in "Boomtown." She was an attractive young woman with a cute accent—a hard worker who easily could handle her GI customers.

She had lost an eye as a child in World War II when Americans bombed Vienna. The horrible destruction and carnage she saw then haunted her dreams for decades after. It also established her suspicious view of life and her tendency to quickly size up people and situations in black and white. She was very frank. She had taught herself English by listening to her customers and watching TV.

In late 1965, she became seriously ill and spent the next several months in a VA hospital. We became close when I wrote and visited her. When she got out, we started dating, fell in love, and planned a new life together. She was divorced and we were married in 1967. We built a house in Sillery Bay, MD and were very happy together. In 1969, I left an illustration job at army recruiting and went to work as a visual information specialist at the IRS National Training Center in Crystal City (Arlington), VA. By 1970, we had a son, David, and then a daughter, Jessica, in 1974.

When I became public affairs officer (PAO) in the IRS Baltimore District in 1973, it was a tumultuous time for the Agency and I was on call 24-7. We moved into a bigger house with a two-car garage and an Olympics-size pool. It was a happy and prosperous time. Things changed in 1979 when I became regional PAO in Philadelphia and we moved to Somerdale, NJ. There I was responsible for public affairs in five Mid-Atlantic states and Washington, D.C.

Susie had never wanted to leave Maryland and the only "family" she had ever known in the states, the Kiriazoglous. Within a few years, with the kids getting older, she became depressed and didn't want to leave the house. The thing that got her out of it was working as a volunteer for NJ Representative Jim Florio. Then she befriended a neighbor who was the sister of Ron

Susie in Fur, 1968 oil, 16" X 20"

Jawarski, quarterback for the Philadelphia Eagles. Ron asked the two of them to run his new golf course, The Eagles Nest, in Sewell, N.J. Hobnobbing with celebrities in a new and exciting world made Susie feel useful again. It also turned her head and eventually destroyed our marriage. In fairness to her, I admit that I had been a workaholic in several demanding jobs and I didn't see it coming. We were divorced in 1986.

Susie was and is an extraordinary woman. Although we went through a difficult, painful separation, we have a good relationship today and have always shared concerns about our children.

Joe Alton

People in Maine are known for being frank and direct, but not as much so as Susie, who was tempered by her childhood experiences in war-torn Vienna and saw most things clearly in black and white.

In the middle years of our marriage, while I was Public Affairs Officer, the IRS Baltimore District was investigating county executives, the Maryland governor, Vice President Agnew, and President Nixon. The probes inevitably got around to our own Anne Arundel County Executive, Joe Alton. Susie had known him for years while working at the Lighthouse. Because of disclosure laws, I couldn't talk about any of these sensitive matters to Susie or anyone else, despite keen media interest. That didn't stop her, though.

I came home one day to have her clearly demonstrate that to me, after IRS investigators were reported to have removed boxes of files from Alton's offices. Susie announced, "We (all constituents) got a letter from Joe Alton today saying he was being investigated and asking whether he should resign. I already answered him," she added.

Beginning to be a little concerned, I said, "Oh, really, what did you say?"

"I told him," she said, "dear Joe, everyone knows you're a crook, but I think you're doing a good job, so I hope you stay in office until you are indicted."

Nazis

I realized her frankness early on at our first IRS Christmas party in Baltimore.

She was chatting in the corner with then District Director William Waters, a black man of utmost integrity who had hired me and was being criticized for a lightweight audit of Nixon's taxes.

Bill was nervously laughing at what could well have been outlandish statements, so I sidled over to pick up the conversation.

"Americans are so stupid," she said. "They think it couldn't happen here, but Nixon is just another Hitler. Those two guys he has working for him, Haldeman and Ehrlichman, are both nothing but Nazis."

Bill found her quite entertaining and took it all in stride. I'm sure he had no love for Nixon, but the President was our big boss, after all. Little did any of us know that, a couple of years later, Watergate would prove she was pretty much right.

"Maine!"

Susie, the kids, and I were driving into Maine from Maryland when we decided to stop for lunch. I was determined not to have just fast food, so I took the exit for Kennebunkport and stopped at a little manned booth. "We want to go into town for some lunch," I said to the guy "so do I turn left down here?"

"Yep," he said.

So we went into town only to find the electricity out. After getting lobster rolls at a hotdog stand and walking around a bit, we went back out and I stopped again at the booth. "By the way," I said, "the whole town is out of electricity."

"Yep," he said, "been out since 'leven a'clock this mawnin'."

"Maine," was all my wife said, rolling her eyes upward.

Another time, I stopped at the Turnpike rest stop and was looking over postcards, many of them about the Bush "Summer White House" in Kennebunkport. One particular card caught my eye, as it was all black with some white writing, which, upon closer inspection, read "Kennebunkport at night."

"Maine humor", I thought.

Staying Fit

I've never been much of a fitness buff. I jogged for a while, until I rationalized that it wasn't good for my knees. I realized in my early thirties that I should be doing more when my Austrian father-in-law visited from Vienna. I came home from work one night and he announced, through Susie, that he had tried on one of my suits and it fit perfectly. I asked how that could be, since I was slim and about six feet tall, while he was much stockier at maybe five foot five. She explained, "Simple. You have the body of a 72-year-old man."

A few years later, during a physical check-up, the doctor said that, if I could get on a regimen of eating healthy and exercising regularly, I could get back the body of a 43-year-old man. "Yeah, but I'm only 38," I protested.

Dave and Jess

Susie and I are very proud of our son and daughter. They have weathered their parents' divorce and succeeded in life with confidence and humor.

David and his talented wife, Colleen, a nutritionist, have made a good life in Mullica Hill, NJ. He has a winning personality and has always been willing to tackle any project or new job. He learned early, in Little League baseball, that life is not always fair, often depending on whether your dad is a friend of the coach, and so forth. When that was repeated in football, he refused, at the age of ten, to give up a defensive position he was really good at for an offensive one he could also do but didn't want, just because of someone else's dad. When he quit the team, the coach came to the house every night for a week to change his mind, but he refused to budge. Although I was very proud to see him play football, I let it be his decision. He stuck by his guns and never played again.

When Dave was about eleven, Susie passed out on the way home from the Echelon Mall, with the kids in the car. She'd pulled over just inside the entrance to our community. A neighbor discovered them and

David at Nine (son), 1978 graphite, 14" X 11"   *Jessica at Four* (daughter), 1978 graphite, 14" X 11"

drove them home, leaving the car there. Susie later gave Dave the keys and asked him to ride his moped back to the car and make sure it was locked. Instead, he lifted the heavy moped into the back of the Gran Torino wagon and drove it the half mile home, passing a cop on the way. Susie almost fainted again when he pulled into the driveway. That night, I asked Dave to take a ride to the store with me, as I wanted to talk to him about what he had done. I started out by saying how proud of him I was for what he had accomplished. Then I was trying to find the words to explain that he should never do something like that again. Instead, I finally blurted out, "Did you have any trouble with the car?"

"No," he said. "She started right up."

* * * * *

On a trip from Maryland to Maine in 1975, Dave had remarkable insights into current events for a boy not yet six. While we were discussing whether Nixon had lied in Watergate and should be fired, Dave observed, "Presidents are like that." Realizing he listened to the news, I asked about Archibald Cox. "Cox is already fired," he said. I asked whether he would want to be pope. "No," he said. "They're dropping like flies." At a Kiriazoglou family gathering later, we were discussing worries about drugs in school, when a commercial came on with a skier saying all he needed for a pick-me-up was a Snickers bar. Dave piped up with, "That and a little Coke."

All heads turned immediately toward him.

* * * * *

Jess expressed a similar feeling a few years later when she said Catholic services would be a lot better if they had a Coke machine. On another trip to Maine, with my mother in the front seat and Dave and Jess in the back of our Ford Torino wagon, Dave suddenly complained that Jess had written a dirty word. He passed the paper to the front; it read, "Dave is a ass." I scolded her and said I didn't want to see any more of that. A few minutes later, Dave said she'd done it again. Sure enough, she had, but this time she wrote, "Dave, you are still a ass."

* * * * *

After my divorce, I picked up Dave and Jess for a movie one night. Jess was talking about the news story of a handsome Philly newscaster who ended up in the emergency room because of some bizarre gay ritual. She asked whether I thought it was true. I tried to explain that whether or not he was gay, that kind of story could ruin a person. "Oh, he's gay all right," she insisted, "You can tell by looking at him."

"Oh, really," Dave interjected. "What does a gay person look like, Jess?"

"He looks like you, Dave," she answered.

* * * * *

Years later, in her more self-absorbed youth, Jessica announced that she didn't plan to have kids.

"Let me guess why not, Jess" I said. "They're a pain in the ass and they cost too much."

"Bingo," she said.

* * * * *

After an early false start, Jessica went back to college while working full time and got her nursing degree from Drexel University in Philly, along with a huge student-loan debt. She loves her nursing job, she's good at it, and she has been recognized many times by her coworkers and patients as extraordinarily caring.

From the time she said "Dada" while I was bathing her at five months, she has always enjoyed talking. Recently, when asked how she comes out with stuff so quickly, she said, "I want to be entertained and surprised, just like everybody else, by the stuff that comes out of my mouth." Ironically, she had just described the way I feel about my new method of improvisational painting.

Finally, I have to include one of her recent comments to show just how funny and perceptive she is. We were discussing some of the main political players in Washington when a certain senator came up, one known for his sheepish look and darting eyes. Here's Jessica's take on him:

"He always looks like he just farted and doesn't want anybody to know it."

"EXACTLY," I thought. My kids and I pretty much see eye to eye on politics.

Uncle Clarence

Clarence Hilyard was a true Renaissance man. He grew up in Fort Fairfield and married my mother's sister Glenda. After a stint in the navy in World War II, he left his hometown so he wouldn't end up a potato man.

He credited his paternal grandfather, for whom he was named, with instilling in him a lifelong confidence that he could handle whatever problems came his way. He was advised as a kid, "You can solve any problem, if you think long enough about it, and if you can think it, you can do it."

That was certainly true of Clarence. He loved to hunt and fish, and he became a taxidermist in order to mount his trophies. He and Aunt Glenda eventually landed in suburban Connecticut with their family, where they were managers in a shoe factory. They gave it all up in the mid 1960s to buy the Katahdin Lake Camps in the wilderness of Maine so he could serve as a guide to hunters and fishermen. Teddy Roosevelt had used one of the cabins there, after he had been toughened up as a youth by one of Clarence's predecessor guides, William Wingate Sewall.

Clarence Hilyard, 1988 oil, 10" x 8"

Indeed, life there was tough, but Clarence's whole family loved it. They had to give it up after four or five years when Glenda's rheumatoid arthritis got really bad. Clarence was offered a manager position in California when he impressed one of his hunting clients with his organizational skills by orchestrating a successful search for a lost hunter.

A few years later, he was in eastern Pennsylvania working for utility contractor Henkels & McCoy, which has crews throughout the Mid-Atlantic States. He laid countless miles of wiring and fiber-optic cable under Philadelphia and the Delaware River for universities, utilities, and other businesses. Early on, he bought his own computer, taught himself how to use it, and programmed his own spreadsheet to project all job costs and come in with the lowest bid. He was prepared for any eventuality. One time Karen expressed concern about her daughter's safety in Philadelphia, and Clarence pulled out a case of mace. He designed and built an electric lift to get Glenda into their camper and a special bed to help her. After he retired, although he had access to heavy equipment, he once moved a heavy slab of slate to the back of his property by himself, using ropes, trees, and a come-along winch,

just to see if he could do it. Not long after, they moved back to Maine.

I lived with them during the week for six months or more in 1979 and '80, while in the midst of a lengthy move from Maryland to South Jersey. Later, he was like a second father to Karen and to me. I told him one time how I admired his attitude in tackling odd jobs. "When I do it," I explained, "I don't have the right tools, it comes with the wrong parts, screws are missing, I have to make a half dozen trips to the store, and I skin my knuckles all to hell."

"That's the way I do it too," he said. Somehow, I felt a lot better.

David Hilyard

Clarence passed that can-do attitude on to his four children. His youngest child, David, and David's then-wife, Darie, worked for several years to polish the surface of the huge mirrors used in the world's largest telescope. The Keck Telescope in Hawaii enables us to see things in deep space for the first time. It's remarkable to me that, without the work of my cousin and his wife, one young couple, all of those images would still be beyond the rest of us on the planet.

James Fitzgerald

One frequent visitor to the isolated Katahdin camps had been the painter James Fitzgerald, largely unknown then but gaining recognition now. Fitzgerald kept to himself, spent a lot of time studying and painting the "moods of the mountain," and preferred to eat in the kitchen with Clarence and Glenda rather than with the hunters.

Glenda, chief cook and bottle washer, once prevailed upon him to freshen up the faded colors on a mounted rainbow trout, but he begged off. She eventually convinced him by promising an apple pie for his troubles. He put it off for a while, but one day he delivered the goods. Glenda was not impressed with the results.

"It was a terrible mess," she said, "all rough and abstract (like his paintings), and didn't look anything like a rainbow trout. It was so bad I had to paint over it myself."

When she finished, she asked Jim what he thought of her painting skills, and he said, "Don't give up your day job, Glenda."

Another time, Fitzgerald was standing alone at the lakeshore smoking his pipe and studying the mountain when a group of hunters came walking into camp. As they got closer to him, they shouted, "Hey, mister, which way to the camps?" He never moved a muscle or let on that he heard. They tried again as they got closer. No reaction from him. Finally, as they got right upon him, they said, "Hey, mister, didn't you hear us calling to you?"

"Can't you see I'm busy?" he said.

Clarence once suggested to Fitzgerald that his paintings didn't look the way the mountain really looked. "No," he answered, "but don't you wish it did look like that?"

That's a painter for you.

Knuckleheads

Clarence and Glenda had a big recreation vehicle and liked to take trips across the country. On one such trip, they met someone with mutual experiences.

They had stopped at a campsite in California and Clarence had wandered up to the common area and got talking to a man who had a similar RV. "Where you from?" the guy wanted to know.

"Maine," he said.

"Oh? Where in Maine?" the guy asked.

"Some place up north you've never heard of," Clarence said.

"I might have," the guy said. "I know Maine."

"Fort Fairfield." Clarence replied.

"Yes, I know right where it is," the guy said. "I was stationed at Loring." Loring Air Force Base was a B-52 SAC base in Limestone, eight miles from Karen's homestead.

"My brother-in-law, Walter, worked on the base many years as a mason," Clarence offered. "He always said the fellows that ran that base were a bunch of knuckleheads" (one of Uncle Walter's favorite expressions).

"Is that right?" the guy answered, then things were quiet for a few minutes.

"What did you do when you were there?" Clarence wanted to know.

"I was the base commander," he said.

Camping

When we were planning to move back to Maine in 2002, Karen called Clarence, who had moved back earlier, to ask how things were here now, compared to Philly.

"Things are probably a lot cheaper," she assumed.

"Not really," he said. "Food and utilities are about the same, and you pay more for heat. See, where you really save is on clothing. There's nothing to do and nowhere to go, so you don't have to buy a lot of clothes. Of course, there's always camping," he added.

"Camping?" she asked incredulously. "Living in Maine is camping."

She had revealed some misgivings about her home state another time, when we were on our way here from Pennsylvania. In her youth, she had been like many young people even today who can't wait to leave their cold state of limited opportunity. Now we had just met or passed several trucks hauling sections of modular homes, which were becoming quite popular with retirees like Clarence.

"I wonder what the deal is with all these doublewides on the road," I asked.

"The people in Maine are so friggin' bored they have to move their houses for something to do," she explained.

Karen

Without listing all the ways I find her attractive and exciting, let me just say that my wife is all of the women I ever loved or ever wanted to love. She couldn't possibly be more loving and supportive. We are sublimely compatible.

She was born in Fort Fairfield two months after me, but, unlike me, she had grown up on a farm with Christian conservative parents, which meant no dances, no movies, no teen parties, and so forth. We were in school together for three years before I moved to Belfast, but we didn't socialize outside of class.

Thirty years later, early in our marriage, I gave her a valentine with Clark Gable and Vivien Leigh on the cover, and she posted it on the wall above her computer. Later, after watching an old movie about the 1906 San Francisco earthquake and fire, starring Gable, she turned to me and asked, "Who was that guy?"

"You're kidding, right?" I asked.

"No," she said. "Who was he? He was kind of good looking."

Karen Smiling, 1988 charcoal, 14" x 12"

Nine O'clock at Night

Karen and I had been in grammar school together in Fort Fairfield, but my family moved to the Maine coast during our freshman year. We reconnected when I went to her 25th high school reunion instead of my own in Belfast.

That day we spent a few hours walking around town getting reacquainted during the Potato Blossom Festival. That night, we hung out together again at the reunion, held at the Fish and Game Club in Puddle Dock. She had changed so much that her classmates didn't know her, and I was happy to introduce her as my date. They thought she was "hot," and I did too. Throughout the evening, she wouldn't drink, except to sip on my scotch, which she didn't like, because she knew her parents would frown on her drinking when she got home.

As has often been the case, I didn't have the good sense earlier in the day to invite her to come with me, so she drove there in her dad's old DeSoto station wagon with a missing muffler. After the reunion, a small gang of us gathered at Winston "Bucky" Marshall's house to sing around the piano and socialize into the wee hours. When Karen drove home, she turned the lights off and coasted into the driveway so as not to wake her parents. Much to her surprise, her mother met her at the door with a cup of coffee and a knowing look. Both had waited up for her.

"Daddy, I'm forty-three years old," she said in exasperation. "I can't believe you waited up for me."

"Nothing good goes on in town after nine o'clock," was his reply.

Marriage

After two years of being inseparable, Karen and I were visiting Maine and had her parents with us on the coast. As we were packing up to leave my mother's upstairs apartment at the Hilltop Birches in Belfast, her mother followed me down to the car.

"You know," she said, "you and Karen ought to do the right thing." When I asked what she meant, she added, "You know, get married."

As I explained that we both had been married before and were being very cautious, I looked at the upstairs window and saw Karen's face, eyes big and wide. She said later she was worried about what her mother was saying to me.

Since I was convinced that Aletha had a direct

line to God, I proposed to Karen a few months later. Within weeks of that, we had gotten married, sold Karen's townhouse in Horsham, and bought a home and studio in Jenkintown, PA. Since then we've lived near Charlotte, NC and are now back in Belfast, ME.

Salem

Maybe one reason Karen and I have been so compatible all these years is that we are distant cousins, going back 10 generations to two sisters hanged as witches in 1692 Salem, MA.

She descended from Rebecca (Towne) Nurse and I descended from Mary (Towne) Estey, two women featured in the movie *The Crucible*, based on Arthur Miller's play. They were later exonerated, largely through the efforts of their younger sister, Sarah Good, who was portrayed by Vanessa Redgrave in PBS's *Three Sovereigns for Sarah*. The state of Massachusetts later denounced the trials.

Karen and I visited the Rebecca Nurse Homestead in what is now Danvers, MA in 2013 and found it a very moving experience. In 2008 I had done an abstract painting about the connection entitled *Salem*.

Yankee

In 1998, we moved with Karen's job at Stabilus to Cramerton, N.C., and built a big, transitional-style home with a large studio in a gated community. We made a lot of good friends over the next four years and enjoyed the warm weather.

One day in January, when it was 69 degrees on our deck, we called friends in Fort Fairfield. It was 30 below zero there. I enjoyed engaging in a wide variety of art activities there with a large circle of artist friends, especially a discussion salon we called The Group, developed from my teaching at Art 1 Gallery in Gastonia. Poor Karen didn't enjoy the South as much as I did because she was working hard night and day. One thing we both noticed: there was a lingering sense of the Civil War. It wasn't always evident but it was often there.

One day I was visiting a little antiques shop in Cramerton, where we lived, and was admiring all of the Civil War items, mostly Confederate. I had been a big student of the Civil War in my youth, and I was telling the shop owner that I had read a lot about it and had drawn dozens of portraits of Abe Lincoln.

"Jist lahk a Yankee," came the cackling voice of a little old lady unnoticed in the back of the store. Actually, I had often drawn John Wilkes Booth and his co-conspirators too, but I wasn't about to get into a conversation with her about it.

Another time, I had The Group over for a studio tour and discussion. One of them, who had deep Southern roots, noticed a striking photo on my wall of General Grant by Mathew Brady, and she quietly commented on it in passing.

"Nice photo, wrong general," she said.

Cecil and Aletha

My in-laws, Cecil and Aletha Emery, were a wonderful, God-fearing farm couple on the Center Limestone Road in Fort Fairfield.

He grew up on a farm and she was a city girl from Marysville, New Brunswick, Canada. Her father was a factory manager with maid service at home. When they got married, they lived in a tent at the farm the first summer and moved into a modified section of the barn for winter—a big change for her.

Aletha was an amazing woman. Her nephew Bill, once described her as the alpha male in the family. She wasn't long gaining and keeping the upper hand throughout her marriage, starting with removing the promise to obey from her wedding vows. She was interested in architecture, new gadgets, photography, home movie–making, and Republican politics. In addition to being bookkeeper for the farm, she was a board member, Sunday-school teacher, and treasurer for the Wesleyan Church and was involved in the Farm Extension Service. She also sold greeting cards, Shaklee Vitamins, and Spencer Corsets (to the nuns in northern Maine)—for which she got an award as top saleslady.

Cecil was much more into animals. He was a simple but very intelligent man who loved books and was an avid reader. He lived most of his life a few miles from where he was born, halfway between Fort Fairfield and Limestone, on the Center Road. He was a potato and dairy farmer up until he had to give up his cows at 72 because of bad knees. He was so upset by it that he had to go to bed. My father once said of him, "If any man deserves to go to heaven, it's Cecil Emery. He's the hardest working man I ever knew." Dad described how Cecil used to come into town and practically run

Cecil Emery, 1989 graphite, 12" x 9"

Aletha Emery, 2000 charcoal, 17" X 14"

104

from store to store so he could get back to his cows. In truth, Cecil was relatively shy and didn't like being in town. When he rode or drove a horse into town for high school, he ate his lunch with the horse.

Cecil and Aletha were both very religious. They lived the Christian life, giving at least ten percent to the Lord in good times and bad. They raised their two girls in the Christian faith and were always inviting churchgoers home to Sunday dinner or taking them in. You couldn't visit there without a big helping of ice cream, which they later got in large containers from Schwan's. Karen can't resist it to this day.

I first met them in 1986, after I started courting Karen. Being strict Wesleyans, they may have been skeptical about my Irish Catholic background, but they accepted me and we became very close when they moved in with us in North Carolina. I looked after them while Karen was still working.

One air force couple they had taken in forty years earlier somehow found them through the local pastor in Carolina and came to visit us there. The couple had dedicated their lives to being missionaries on an Indian reservation in the Southwest. While we were sitting up late talking one night, the husband said Cecil had inspired him to the calling by his example those many years before, and thanked him for a worthwhile life.

Nicollette

Cecil was very much into reflexology and often used it successfully on Aletha to bring her out of her spells (mini strokes). We told him about Nicollette, who knew reflexology; plus she was an acupuncturist and nutritionist with a unique way of identifying things that were toxic to individuals. So when Cecil scheduled a visit to Pennsylvania from Maine, he had to meet Nicollette.

They hit it off right away, as she was an attractive younger woman with a French accent and her father was a well-known French chemist who developed blue vitro, or copper sulfate, which Cecil and most farmers had used to kill potato insects. Her unique method of detecting toxins was to attach to your finger wires that were connected to a German machine that looked like an old telephone switchboard, which could read your reaction to containers of various substances.

Karen and I had been convinced of the machine's validity when Nicollette could detect that we had indulged in a glass of wine the night before.

When we took Cecil and Aletha to see her, Karen

and I first went through the test to show how it worked. Cecil was fascinated with Nicollette and the machine. When she hooked up Aletha, she got no reaction and couldn't read her despite repeated tries. So she decided that, since she already had my readings, she would hook me up, have me hold Aletha's hand, and read the differences. It seemed to work really well. "Oh, yes, I'm getting a very strong reading now," Nicollette announced.

"Whew, I'm getting warm," Aletha exclaimed.

"Yes, I'm getting a very good reading," Nicollette injected. Cecil leaned in from the rear with great interest.

"I'm sweating," Aletha said, "and I never sweat."

"Pigs are like that," Cecil offered. Aletha just rolled her eyes upward, but Nicollette nearly fell off her chair with laughter.

Mules

Cecil loved horses and mules. As a kid, he drove them on his grandfather's farm. In fact, he deeply regretted the day when they were replaced by tractors.

When we moved him at age 85 to North Carolina, 1500 miles away from the only home he had ever known, we worried about his becoming depressed. I found that one way to prevent that was to find a mule we could visit. That was easy enough in Carolina. You could cruise the suburbs of Charlotte and quite often come across a mule standing in a carport. I found seven of them in close proximity to our home, so we would make the rounds every few days, preceded by a stop at Krispy Kreme for donuts and coffee. What could be better?

I really grew to love my in-laws once they moved in with us. They liked our new, modern home in the gated community, where they had their own bedroom, bathroom, and den. But it wasn't perfect, according to Cecil. He often told people at my art openings, "They have enough room for a mule out back, but they have a lot of funny rules there." He also didn't see why he couldn't take a leak in the front yard after dark, which mortified his daughter.

Lucy the Cow

While Cecil and Aletha were with us in North Carolina, I ran across an article in the paper about a champion cow that gave far more milk than perhaps any other cow in recorded history. I knew I had to take Cecil to see her.

Lucy routinely produced around 200 lbs. of milk a day, two and a half times that of the average Holstein. When we traveled to Cleveland County to see her, we learned that all she did all day was eat, drink, and produce milk, and that she rarely lay down. We had a nice visit with her young owners, Terry and Sarah Foster, and got several pictures. Cecil was in his glory.

Her lineage was especially intriguing. The couple had gotten her from a local herd that belonged to the Nutters, a family that had come down from Maine. A Nutter family in southern Maine had gotten many of its best cows from Cecil's brother Carl. He had gotten much of his prize stock from Cecil. While we weren't able to prove it, we harbored the notion that the best-producing milk cow in the world could be traced back to Cecil's Holsteins in Fort Fairfield.

Chinese Food

Cecil was a meat-and-potatoes guy, not given to trying fancy foreign food. While he was living with us in Carolina, we had Chinese food one night. He ate it but I saw that he wasn't crazy about it. "What do you think of the Chinese food?" I asked.

"Well, I wouldn't go all the way to China for it," he replied. So I guessed that from then on we should stick to beans, pancakes, and potatoes. "Stop right there," he said.

I have to say, though, that he did like to go to the Shogun Japanese steakhouse, where they grilled the food right in front of us. When asked where he might like to eat out, he would say, "Let's go to that place where they set the food on fire."

Chocolates

Cecil loved sweets, especially chocolates, like his daughter Karen. While he was with us in Carolina, one of her friends brought us a box of chocolates for Christmas. Cecil couldn't wait to get into them, but Karen warned him that we were about to eat. "Now Daddy, don't you dare eat those chocolates before dinner." He agreed reluctantly.

While we were all engaged in Christmas chatter, Karen noticed that someone had been into the chocolates, and she knew exactly who. "Daddy," she said rather sharply, "you've eaten three of those chocolates already."

"No I haven't," he said.

"Yes, you have, Daddy. There are three empty

wrappers there," she said.

"I've got three in my mouth, but I haven't eaten them," he said.

Job

In his late years, Cecil definitely showed signs of dementia. Yet, his mind was still very active and curious. Before moving with us to North Carolina, Karen's daughter Tammy, had been caring for her grandparents in northern Maine and reported that often he couldn't remember how to button his shirt. After the move, he showed wonderful improvement with the drug Exelon.

One morning, in his mid-eighties, he was perusing the local want ads when he announced, "I think I'm going to find a job."

Aletha quickly threw cold water on that idea. "Cecil, how are you going to get to a job? You can't even find the bathroom."

He was just as quick to respond. "David will take me."

Years earlier, his oldest sister, Mae, mother of Uncle Clarence Hilyard and the caretaker for many in the family over the years, had shown the same characteristic grit and work ethic. On his last visit to see his bedridden mother in a nursing home, Clarence was about to go out the door after saying goodbye when his mother called to him. "Clarence," she said. As he stopped and turned, she asked, "You don't know where I can get a job, do you?"

Six Legs

My in-laws had a long and loving relationship, even though they were quite different in many ways.

Once, during lunch in North Carolina, Aletha became annoyed at Cecil because he wouldn't stop talking while she was trying to listen to Rush Limbaugh on the radio. "Cecil, please, I'm trying to hear this," she said.

Seeing that he was getting to her, he continued in a teasing way, adding, "You know what I think of that."

"What?" she asked.

"What Karen always says," he replied.

"What does Karen always say?" she asked.

"Bullshit," he replied, and kept on talking.

"Cecil," she began again, "if you don't stop talking, I'm going to leave the room." He kept talking. Suddenly, she got up and started out of the room with her four-pronged walker on wheels, necessitated by a recent hip operation.

Just as she got to the hallway, Cecil called out, "Letha."

"What is it, Cecil?" she asked, showing her annoyance.

"You're the best-looking six-legged walker in this house," he exclaimed. She melted into a smile as she turned the corner, out of sight.

Drawing Lesson

Cecil had endless interests and curiosity, even in his late eighties. One day in Carolina he announced that he'd like to learn to draw. Since I was conducting a basic drawing workshop that next Saturday at Art 1 Gallery in Gastonia, I invited him to come along.

While I was going through some preliminary information, I noticed him exploring the provided materials, including a chunk of charcoal wrapped in cellophane, which he thought was candy and bit into. He quickly recovered from his mistake and set about drawing. Since I hadn't finished my introductory remarks or taught anything yet, I was curious to go around later to see what he had been doing. He had drawn a few childlike renderings of things he knew: a cat, his beagle ("Skitter," as he called her), a pig, and three very-nicely-drawn potatoes. In fact, as a tribute to him, I later included those potatoes in a large painting of a potato field called *Aroostook*, on the cover and now hanging at the University of Maine Hutchinson Center in Belfast.

Cecil looked around the circle of drawing participants and landed on one attractive young woman who was very animated and abstract in her drawing. Pretty soon, he got up and went around behind her to watch what she was doing. Here's where he often could be very surprising. Although he had spent his whole life in very quiet, conservative circles, had very little experience with art, and knew next to nothing about abstract art, he suddenly came out with, "I like the way you think."

When we got home, he very proudly took out that first effort to show Aletha. She immediately burst into fits of laughter that she couldn't seem to stop. She later apologized but couldn't keep herself from laughing every time she gazed upon his work. Long after, just mentioning it would bring on the same reaction. Poor Cecil. He took it all very well.

Redfoot

One of my artist friends in North Carolina was Darlene Redfoot (her married name). Cecil was quite intrigued with the idea that she might be an Indian. What followed was Cecil and Aletha's version of the Abbot and Costello routine of "Who's on first?"

"Redfoot, Redfoot," he pondered one morning. "I think she might be an Indian."

"Who?" Aletha asked.

"Redfoot," he said again.

"She reminds me of Terry," Aletha offered.

"Who's Terry?" he asked.

"Oh, you know Terry," she said. "The one who used to walk with Tammy back home."

"Oh," he said. Then, upon further reflection, he said, "Letha, let me ask you something."

"What?" she said.

"What makes you think she's an Indian?" he asked.

"Who?" she said.

"Terry," he said. "What makes you think she's an Indian?"

"I never said she was an Indian," she replied.

"Oh," he said. "I thought you said she was an Indian."

Pictures

After Cecil and Aletha had lived with us a few years, it was decided that they would go to live for a while with their other daughter, Gilda, in Dubuque, Iowa. In preparation, they decided to pare down their lifetime of old photos kept in two big popcorn canisters.

They agreed that each would go through them independently and pick out the ones to be saved. Cecil selected and saved all the pictures of horses and cows, which he fondly identified by name, and he threw out pictures of kids and churchgoers he couldn't remember. Aletha went through and saved all of the pictures of people, most of whom she remembered well, and threw out all the pictures of animals. So after two days of sorting out pictures, they put them all back together and filled the two canisters back up for shipment to Iowa.

Ruckus

After we returned home to Carolina after burying Cecil in northern Maine, the mailman stopped me to say that he had one more Cecil story I didn't know.

He and his wife had come from a dairy farm in Vermont, and she was a hospice volunteer, so they had seemed like a logical couple to parent sit with Cecil and Aletha while Karen and I enjoyed a much-needed getaway to Charleston and Savanna. They were willing, so we invited them to dinner, just to see how compatible the four would be. Everything worked out great, since Cecil charmed them with his photo albums of the farm and his endless stories.

So the postman said to me, "You remember that weekend we stayed with Cecil and Aletha? Well, Cecil, couldn't wait to get us upstairs to your studio. Remember that you had a lot of nude drawings all over the walls? We were up there about an hour looking around, with Cecil walking along with his hands behind his back, not saying a thing. Later, while we were having dinner, he suddenly spoke up out of the blue."

As the postman told it, Cecil said: "If all them people upstairs ever get loose, there's going to be quite a ruckus up there."

Republican

Aletha liked to follow politics. She was a strong Republican, often made contributions to the party, and listened to right-wing talk shows, like Rush Limbaugh's. I recall often seeing Senator Olympia Snow veer off to the side in a parade to say hello to Letha. Her loyalty to the party is evident in the following story.

Ron Dow was a longtime friend of the family in Aroostook and had recently moved to Belfast when we saw him at an art opening after Aletha had passed. He noticed that Karen wore an Obama button.

"Your mother would roll over in her grave if she saw that," he grinned. "I remember the time I noticed a political sign on her lawn and I told her that the guy was a real jerk."

"I know," she had replied, "but he's a Republican."

Banana

Aletha spent her last summer with us in 2005 in Belfast. Karen was still working for MBNA, so I looked after Aletha during the day. She was 92, nearly blind with macular degeneration, and suffering from dementia.

One morning she called to me from upstairs before I had a chance to bring up her pills and banana. She was clearly upset.

"I need some help," she said frantically, "in the bathroom. I've been working as fast as I can but I can't keep up."

"What's in the bathroom?" I asked.

"The job, all those bottles," she said. "I can't keep

up. Get me some help!"

"There's nothing in the bathroom," I said. "You're just imagining things."

"No, I'm not," she said. "I need some help!"

Thrown off balance by the situation, I desperately tried to think of something to bring her back to reality. "Would you like a banana?" I asked.

"Don't be silly," she said, her black eyes flashing. "GET ME SOME HELP!"

I finally convinced her that we could straighten out the situation when Karen came home, and we went down for breakfast.

"Yes," she said, "Karen will know what to do."

She had a lot of confidence in Karen, but one morning she didn't know her own daughter. Karen said her mother seemed to have reverted back to being a little girl. Yet when Venus, one of our English bulldogs, came up the stairs to see what was happening, Aletha said, "Good morning, Venus."

A few months later, when Aletha was back in Iowa with her older daughter, Gilda, and was dying, Karen flew out to be with her. When she saw Karen, she said, "Everything will be straightened out now. Karen's here."

Aletha died a few weeks later, in February 2006.

Near Misses

I've had several episodes that I think of as near-death experiences.

Once as a kid, I was playing king of the mountain with Tommy Gagnon and some others on a snowbank down over the C & P Railroad yard at the Fort. Somebody pushed me off the top and I was sliding down head first on my back, just as a truck loaded with potatoes was pulling in right below me. I grabbed at the packed snow and tried frantically to stop. I saw the front tires pass by me and the double tires on the loaded back end coming straight for my head. Suddenly I stopped, and the big tires rolled over the hair on the back of my head.

Little did I know that Dad had been watching from across the street and was waiting anxiously to see if that kid would come back up over the snowbank. He told the story at supper that night and said his heart leaped to his throat when the face that appeared was mine.

* * * * *

Years earlier, we had been coming back from Plaster Rock, N.B., and Dad was driving when someone said the back door, which opened out to the wind in that car, was not shut tight. "I'll get it," I said, and reached over from my middle seat to close it. The wind and speed yanked me halfway out of the car before Uncle Bruce grabbed me around the waist and pulled me back in.

* * * * *

My father often drove around on "slicks" in the winter—no snow tires, chains, studs, or even good tread, so this next one is partially his own fault. One night while in high school, I had dropped off my date, Joanne Boynton, at Board Landing and was just rounding a steep hill on outer High Street in Belfast, but Dad's big, white Mercury Monterey started spinning, couldn't make it, slid off the road, and was sliding backwards down glare ice toward the Passagassawakeag River. I thought the car and I were both goners, until a back tire fetched up on a nub of ice. I carefully got out of the car but left the lights on so people would see it, then I half crawled up the hill to the Jenks's house. Luckily, some men with a tractor were able to pull me out, and I drove home. As I was approaching the house, at the corner of Grove and Congress Streets, the car died and I coasted to a stop on the shoulder. Since it was spring and the beginning of what we call "mud season," the car sank to the frame.

Next morning Dad didn't see the car up in the driveway, so he asked me where it was. I told him it was down front and I would show him why. When he learned that it was sunk up to the frame in mud with a dead battery, he wasn't too pleased.

"You don't know the half of it," I said. Then I told him the rest of the story.

* * * * *

On October 25, 1972, while working in Crystal City, VA, I had scheduled a 10 a.m. meeting with the bank manager of Arlington Trust across the plaza to discuss a loan for a vacation trip to Austria. As the time approached, I looked down from my office window and saw that some telephone workmen were down in a manhole outside. Shortly thereafter, I heard all kinds of sirens and commotion centering on the bank.

It turned out that the workmen were frauds who had cut the telephone and alarm lines to the bank as part of a robbery in progress. Charles Tuller, two sons, and a fourth accomplice ended up killing the bank manager, Harry Candee, and a police officer in their failed attempt. They then fled to Houston, Texas, and hijacked an Eastern Airlines jet to Cuba. Three years later, they sneaked back into the U.S., were arrested or turned themselves in, and were imprisoned.

Had I gone to the bank a little early, I would have been in harm's way, if not possibly killed. In the end, I did get the loan and we did vacation in Vienna.

* * * * *

Karen had her own near miss in 1952, the year the ice-out destroyed the pavement-covered wooden deck of the old Fort Fairfield bridge. She and other schoolchildren on the north side of the Aroostook River were taken by bus to the bridge and led across by hand. In the process she fell into an open space just above the rushing, ice-filled waters and was grabbed at the last minute by the bus driver—it may have been Sherman Brayall—who saved her life. She has been afraid even to ride over bridges ever since, sometimes closing her eyes the whole way.

* * * * *

In recent years, Karen and I had a very disconcerting close call. We were somewhere near Albion, coming back to Belfast from Waterville. We were going about 50 miles an hour on a main road when a car shot across the road, immediately in front of us, going at about the same speed. It would have been fatal, and all the more surprising to surviving friends and family because they had no idea we'd been there.

* * * * *

Most recently, while I was working on this book, I suffered a very painful 25-day ordeal with kidney stones. In the process, I had several procedures, a severe septic infection, and lost 25 lbs. At one point, Karen insisted that we go to the emergency room at Waldo County General Hospital. When the doctor saw me, he later admitted to Karen, he wasn't sure I would make it. It is hard to believe that such a small item can cause so much pain and be so dangerous.

God has smiled upon us over and over, sometimes just in the nick of time.

Mom's Passing

My mother's death in 1987 was a very spiritual event for me. We came home to Belfast after she had suffered a stroke, was in a coma and was near death.

I think she waited until we got here, because she went downhill fast after squeezing my hand to acknowledge my presence. My sisters were with us when I asked in prayer that God revive her, if it was His will, or help her through a peaceful transition, if she was ready. Since we didn't expect her to survive the night, Barb, who had cared for her in recent years, couldn't bear to stay. She and Alana left with Karen. Cheryl and I wanted to stay. We sat, held Mom's hand, and watched the life flow out of her.

Shortly after midnight, I think, she opened her eyes and looked directly at me, almost through me, with a beatific smile on her face. Then she closed her eyes and stopped breathing. Cheryl and I both felt privileged to have been there.

Best of Show

Dad wasn't given to openly complimenting me—not for my success in high school, my college honors program in Italy, my successful government career, or my advances in fine-arts painting.

Nevertheless, I know he was proud of my accomplishments. First of all, he had enough faith in me that, despite personal misgivings and his not having saved any money for my further education, he let me and my high-school advisors decide where I would go to college—RISD. Secondly, I retired from my government career at the top of a grade 14, whereas he had been a grade nine as county agent. Of course, my college degree made a lot of difference, and I had my career in a different place and time.

It was years later that his approval regarding my artwork became particularly sweet. To put it in context, Dad had never thought fine-arts painting was a very promising career. He was right. He also didn't understand or appreciate my evolving from competent portraiture and landscapes to abstraction. During a visit to Melberg Gallery, one of the best in Charlotte, NC, he stood in front of an abstract piece and said, "Now, I suppose you like that."

"I love it," I said.

"I hate it," he replied.

During another visit, it turned out that I was in three competitive shows opening within one week. He went with us to all three openings. I took the first prize at Lincoln Cultural Center in Lincolnton, then the best of show at the Schiele Museum in Gastonia, and the $500 purchase prize at the Charlotte Art League. While they called out the place prizes in Charlotte, Karen was standing behind Dad and said he had his fingers crossed. When I wasn't named, he seemed disappointed. Then they named my piece the best of show. It was sweet, not only because Dad was there, but because the abstract piece was called *Catholic*, because Dad and I had our picture taken in front of it for *Carolina Arts* magazine, and because about a month later a niece in Maine called out to my sister, "Mom, Grampy and Uncle Dave are on the Internet!" It was that picture.

As a footnote, the law firm that furnished the purchase prize later got into litigation with the Catholic Church and didn't feel right about displaying my piece, so they gave it back to me and never picked out a replacement. I still have it.

Dad did give me a very nice direct compliment not long before he died. He was in our house in Maine when I brought out a very realistic painting of a red dogwood up the hill. He studied it carefully for some time, then said, "I'll tell you one thing, you're one hell of a painter."

He also told me right before he died that he was very proud of all of his kids.

Mom never complimented us much either. I knew she was proud of my various achievements by overhearing her in the next room bragging to family and friends.

Rabbit

Like a lot of elderly people, Dad began to say whatever he wanted, anywhere and at any time, often being insensitive to others' feelings.

My neighbor came over one night to cry on my shoulder about his treatment by the town cops. He had been attracting little kids at the local park with his pet rabbit, parents were complaining, and the cops had visited him two nights in a row. I advised him to leave

Catholic, 2000 charcoal, 21" x 32"

the rabbit home when he went to the park, but he didn't listen. Dad was there and took in the whole thing.

Not long after, I was having breakfast at Dudley's diner with Dad and his new and devoted friend, Mac Small, when the neighbor came in and sat a few tables away. "See that guy, Mac," Dad said in a too-loud voice. "People around town call him a queer because he has a rabbit."

I tried to get Dad to pipe down, all to no avail. "So let that be a lesson to you, Mac," he said even louder. "If you don't want people to call you a queer, don't get a rabbit."

Edema

Dad suffered and eventually died from congestive heart failure. He was sometimes cantankerous in the process but he never lost his sense of humor.

He lived in Northport with Barbara the last few years, so she bore the brunt of his belligerence. The last time I had to go down in the night to get him up off the floor, his feet and legs were badly swollen. "That's that edema," Barb kept saying somewhat anxiously.

Randy on Blue, 2001 charcoal & Conte, 20" X 13"

"Barbara," he finally said rather sharply, "don't say that word again." When she asked what word, he said, "That goddamned edema." She did her best.

We took him to the emergency room. He was concerned but still in good spirits. His new doctor, Todd Stapley, came in and asked if he could take a peek down there under the sheet.

"Go ahead," Dad said, "but you're not going to see much." Doctor Stapley had told Dad gently but unmistakably a few weeks earlier what he could expect from now on. When he left the room that time, Dad had said, "He looks like a goddamned kid but he's a smart son of a bitch."

This time, Dad expressed less confidence. "My mother lived to be 102," he told the doctor. "Oh, I don't expect to live that long, but I would like to make it to my birthday in a few weeks, if you guys don't kill me."

"That's very perceptive," the doctor said with a smile. Dad jerked his head in his direction, eyes as big as saucers.

A male nurse came in and asked Dad if he could give him a shot. Dad eyed the needle, which looked about four inches long, and asked if he was any good at it.

"I think, if you ask around, you'll find that I'm one of the best pricks around here," he said. He was the kind of nurse Dad liked to kibitz with.

There was another one at Harbor Hill, where we got Dad settled in a few months later. He was telling us that she was a little rough but had a great sense of humor, which he really appreciated. Just then, she came in and Dad tried to get a rise out of her with some remark.

"I'll slap your bony ass," she said. Dad laughed heartily.

"God, she's a corker," he said when she left the room.

He died there not long after.

Numb

It's funny how, no matter how old you get, your parents can always put you in your place, just as they did in childhood.

It happened to me on one of the last days with my dying father. We knew he didn't have much longer in his struggle with congestive heart failure. He was in Harbor Hill rehab center just across the footbridge from me in Belfast, and was being given morphine for pain. I was spending his last days with him, and we had some time for closure. I did several sketches of him and jotted down some of our conversation in my sketchbook. This was one of the reasons I had moved back to Maine after 42 years away.

At one point in our discussions, he said rather sharply, "Take that thing off the wall over there."

"Where?" I asked.

"Right there behind you on the wall. Get it off," he said.

"There's nothing on the wall there," I said.

"Yes, there is," he insisted. "Can't you see that?"

"Dad, there is nothing there," I explained. "You're just hallucinating from the drugs."

"Numb! Jesus, he's numb," he said.

I immediately reverted back to being a little boy, stung by my father's disapproval. I knew that he was well aware of my success in life and that he was very proud of me. But in his moment of panic and inability to think clearly, I was still his awkward little boy.

Parents always retain a certain stature in our minds, and they wield that power over our emotions, no matter how old we get or how we rationalize that relationship.

Dad's Passing

My father's death, 16 years after Mom's, was not as peaceful but similar. Karen and I had moved back to Belfast a year before, largely because he had not been well. I got to spend a good final year with him before he died. In the final days we had a chance to talk about our lives over the years and say what we needed to say.

On his last day I had been with him for several hours when Karen came in and suggested I take a break, go home, check on our little bulldog, Buddy, and let her sit

When Dad stopped breathing, Barb was on one side holding his hand and Karen was on the other, doing the same. When I came back a few minutes later, he was already gone.

Rainbows

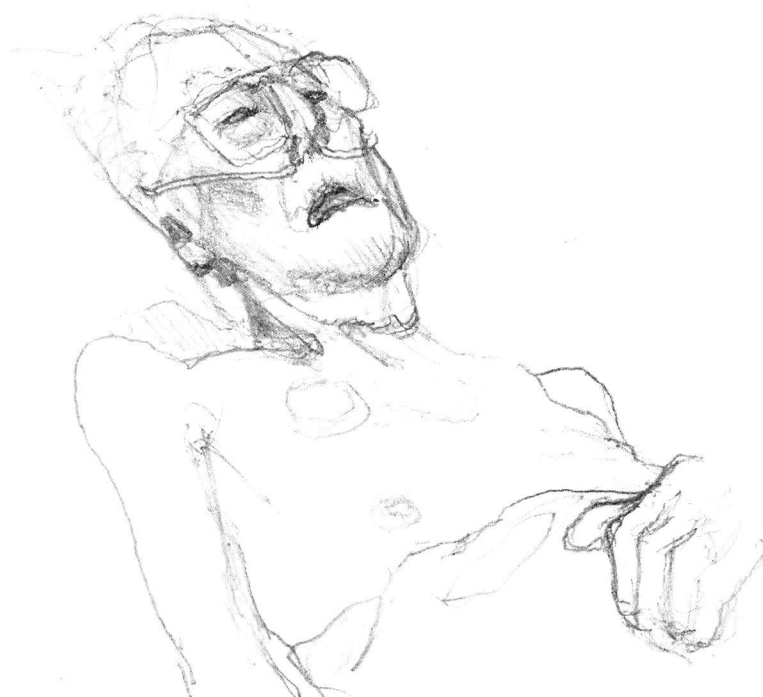

Dad Near the End, 2003 graphite, 4" X 4"

Celestial phenomena have loomed large in our lives in recent years, all around losses in Karen's family.

It all started in the fall of 2001. Cecil was in a coma after a fall in Iowa, and we had scheduled a flight from Charlotte, NC to Dubuque. He died a few hours before we left. As we were ascending from the airport, the city lay below us like sparkling diamonds on a black field, with a thin rim of red on the horizon, a clear blue sky just beginning above it, and one lone star shining brightly high above. We had never seen anything like it and we took it as some sort of sign. It was so memorable that I later did a painting commemorating it called *Ascension*.

in for me a while. Shortly after I left, Barb, who had cared for both Mom and Dad during their last few years, got off work and came in. I think Dad was waiting for her. When she told him it was okay to let go, he did.

Later, we all flew to Bangor and drove together

to Aroostook for his burial. As we reached the County line, a heavy thunderstorm gave way to a bright, late afternoon sun behind us, shining on the hills of Canada in front of us, at the peak of their gold and red fall colors and against a dark green-black sky. Suddenly, a strong double rainbow appeared in front of our path. The whole scene was just spectacular and highly unusual. As if that weren't enough, the dark clouds opened a little hole to reveal a rich turquoise sky beyond and a lone pink cloud peering out. "Hi, Daddy," Karen exclaimed. Indeed, it seemed so. I also did a painting of this memory as a tribute to Cecil, and called it *Resurrection*.

Four years later, on our way to pick up Aletha at the Bangor airport for what turned out to be her last summer with us, we encountered another double rainbow in Frankfort. Karen took it as a welcome from Cecil. A half year later, as I was dropping Karen off at the same airport on her way to see her dying mother in Iowa, a cold, February rain broke to reveal a strong double rainbow, right in the dead of winter.

A couple of years after that, my son, David, and his wife, Colleen, picked us up in Belfast on their way to business in Fort Fairfield. We had a great day together, stopping by the Emery homestead, which we were trying to sell. On the way back, we told them all about the rainbows. Coming down from Bangor, we ran into heavy rain, but as we approached Belfast, the clouds broke, the late afternoon sun shone brightly, and a strong double rainbow appeared behind us.

In 2013, after Karen had returned from giving three weeks of hospice care to her sister in Iowa and right after Gilda had passed, a rainbow of colors appeared on the floor at the top of our stairs. It was caused by the sun passing through Karen's Plexiglas Unsung Hero award from Stabilus, which stood next to Cecil's statue of a black stallion.

We had lived here eleven years and had never seen that happen before.

Gilda and Joel

I didn't see my sister-in-law and her husband very often or get to know them well, because they lived in Iowa.

I remember Gilda from high school. She was a senior when we were freshmen, and she was known as "the brain." In fact, that's what attracted them to one another. After studying medicine in college, she had spent two years in Borneo with the Peace Corps. They were both brilliant and a very nice couple, but the rest of the family affectionately noted that they were not especially aware of or concerned about the practical world around them. They adopted two beautiful daughters, Roseanne and Valerie, and then Gilda gave birth to another, Melissa. Gilda died of cancer in 2013, after Karen spent weeks helping Joel and the girls administer hospice care. Karen really misses her big sister, who was always her protector in their youth.

Joel Samuels had become the library director at the University of Dubuque. Before he retired, he oversaw construction of a beautiful new library and published an extensive book on the university's history. He often engaged me in a remarkably perceptive discussion about art. Like Gilda, his mind often seemed somewhere else.

One time, after a long trip from Iowa to northern Maine in their new car, Joel was walking around the yard with his father-in-law when Cecil suddenly asked, "What kind of car is that?"

"I don't know," Joel said, matter-of-factly.

Later on, Cecil amusingly asked of no one in particular, "What kind of man doesn't know what kind of car he drives?"

Thirty-Seven

I'm very grateful that Karen's grown kids, Tammy, Rocky (Bob), and Ruth Ann, have been so accepting and supportive. They have taken me in, made me part of their family, and shown me great affection and respect. I love them as my own.

Years ago, while the girls were riding with me through Jenkintown, PA, they got onto the subject of their father (Robert Gockley II), the second family he had started, and their new little half brother, David. Ruthie was describing the scenario when David would start school and the teacher would ask whether he had any brothers and sisters—and how old they were.

"Thirty-seven …" she started to say, when Tammy abruptly cut her off.

"I'm not thirty-seven," she said adamantly.

Toilet Training

A humorous incident with my own grandson, Nathan, reminds me of one almost half a century ago that should have prepared me.

George Kiriazoglou was a good husband and father, if a lot like Archie Bunker. He owned and operated the bar and restaurant outside Fort Meade, MD, where my first wife worked. We saw a lot of him and his family.

His wife, Evelyn, informed him one day that he had to talk to their youngest child, Jimmy, who was peeing all over the toilet on his bathroom trips. George agreed and was about to accompany Jim on the next trip when she quietly warned her husband to be gentle. He assured her that he would.

Once inside, Jimmy got started and the problem became very clear to George.

"Jesus Christ, Hoss," he shouted. "Hold that son of a bitch down."

End of problem.

Decades later, I had a similar but quieter experience with Nathan. He and his older sister, Anna Estey Gockley (my namesake), are the children of Karen's son, Robert Gockley III, and his beautiful Russian-born wife, Beatrice. Both kids are beautiful and brilliant, like their parents.

We had gone down to Hatboro, PA and rented an efficiency apartment near their home over the Christmas holidays. The second day we were there, Anna and Nathan were dropped off to spend some time with us. When Nathan, who was three, announced he had to pee, I decided to go in with him.

The first thing he did inside was look in the toilet bowl, where, much to his dislike, he discovered a couple of brown stains. "Kahkah," he said.

Seeing that it bothered him, I explained, "No, it's not. It's just a rust stain."

"Kahkah," he said again.

"No, it's not," I insisted. "Look, I'll flush the toilet and it will still be there." He wasn't convinced. "Well, never mind that," I said, and sat him up there. He dutifully leaned over, looked down and watched the process. When he finished, there was one drop on the end of his tiny weewee. Not sure how to deal with it, I foolishly said, "Shake that thing or bang it."

Being a chip off the old block, who always did things in a big way, he brought the palm of his hand down hard on his knee, BAM, and the drop fell off.

"Are you finished?" I asked. He leaned way over, looked down, and saw that another drop had formed. BAM, he repeated. The second drop fell off. He leaned over again and saw that none had replaced it.

"Okay," he said, "I'm finished."

Second Career

As you have seen, I have been making art one way or another for 65 years. No matter where I was or what job I had at any given time, I was making art.

I began with those many third-grade drawings of experiences and stories, moving on to endless drawings of animals, geological structures, historical figures, movie stars, friends and family, decorative art, and signage. I taught myself to draw and paint, with Norman Rockwell as my inspiration. By the time I went to RISD, I could already draw and paint very well.

From RISD I learned to expand the possibilities of what art could be. Afterward, in the army, I explored the world of illustration, copywriting, and advertising. I also practiced the art of portraiture. At IRS I honed my skills as a photographer, writer, newsletter editor, and PR professional. Once I retired from IRS in 1995, I was free to draw and paint just for me.

In 1994, after ten years of night classes at Pennsylvania Academy of the Fine Arts, I began exhibiting my art in earnest. I have now lived, painted, taught, exhibited, and sold artwork around Baltimore/

Washington, Philadelphia, PA; Charlotte, NC and midcoast Maine. I have produced over 10,000 pieces of art. In the last 20 years, I have had 20 solo exhibits, been in over 30 group and juried exhibits, earned 13 first-place awards, and been the subject of over 70 articles and interviews. My work is in institutions and private collections in 18 states and seven countries. To see more of it and books on my art, visit my website at **www.davidestey.com**.

The Gap

Although I have produced a lot of art, I also lost 30 years in my artistic career by not painting or concentrating on art every day. While I wouldn't give up my government experiences during those years and they do inform the art I make today, that is a big gap in my artistic development that is hard to make up—one half of my adult life. So I've ended up having two full and separate careers. The only thing for me to do at this point is to keep painting, as long as I have the urge to create. Let's see what comes of it. After all, Van Gogh created virtually all of his great work in the last several years of his shortened life.

I like the name David. I understand it to mean "Beloved" and "messenger of God." I feel I have been given a special gift and I am compelled to use it. Critical acclaim may come or not. It doesn't matter

Woman with Comb
(detail), acrylic &
graphite, 18" X 24"

Losing Barb

In the midst of finishing this memoir, I lost my sister Barbara (Mosher), to congestive heart failure, the same ailment that took Dad and at about the same age we lost Mom, 71. It is impossible to honor and summarize a complex life in a few brief paragraphs, but Barb and I have been especially close from early childhood, so I have to include a few thoughts. In many ways, she did not have an easy life. She lost her second daughter, Melissa, in an untimely and inexplicable death at age 15. Barb was married and divorced twice. She took care of Mom and Dad in their failing years, and she suffered vicariously with the many abused and disadvantaged acquaintances, clients and friends she saw over the years while working for Midcoast Mental Health and Coastal Opportunities. Yet she also took great pleasure and pride in her first daughter, Kimberly Nardone, four handsome and talented grandchildren, and six beautiful and promising great grandchildren.

It is amazing and ironic that the beautiful, curly-haired, dimpled and pudgy little girl turned out to look and act so much in her late years like the father whose approval she always sought, while retaining the sweet

David and Barbara at Cheney Grove

smile of Mom's twin sister, Madeline. It seemed strange that she was leaving, while the rest of us went about our business as usual. An odd anxiety, queasiness and heavy weight seemed to hang over the steady stream of family and friends who came to pay tribute to her lifelong friendliness and her steadfast bravery in facing the end. We are all deeply saddened with profound grief at her untimely passing.

So my first real playmate, who became Dale Evans to my Roy Rogers, is gone. When the end finally came, I experienced a flood of emotions, but somewhere in the back of my mind I was always thinking, "Happy trails to you, Barb, until we meet again."

Politics

As I draw this memoir to a close, I think back over the innocence of my youth and worry about the kind of world my grandchildren will face.

When I grew up, children clearly knew the difference between right and wrong and believed that everything would turn out okay if they worked hard and did the right thing. Even in my career, the people I worked with at all levels of government were hard-working public servants. They had great integrity and believed in the righteousness of American democracy. I'm not so sure that is true anymore.

Lately I've begun writing op-ed pieces about the dangerous decline of our democratic process. It is obvious that corporations and the super rich have a stranglehold on our dysfunctional government. It no longer seems capable of making the right decisions on major problems that confront us. Everything is driven by obscene profits. Unless we turn that around, the America we've known and loved cannot endure.

Yet, I have faith that things will change. America has faced seemingly insurmountable challenges throughout history and triumphed over them, but only through difficult and sustained efforts by the people. Countless grassroots efforts already are emerging through the Internet to awaken the electorate and strengthen our better nature.

I believe we are on the verge of great reforms here and around the world. The process may be painful and lengthy, but the results will be a much better place for our grandchildren and for people everywhere.

BAM

Okay, I'm done.

No matter where I've been or what I've done, I've always considered myself a County boy. My family heritage, the Aroostook work ethic and that sometimes-hard environment have shaped my approach to life, from Cheney Grove to Europe, from government to the art world. All of this has never been far from my mind, and I know I have been truly blessed.

I guess this is as good a place as any to end this memoir, with deep appreciation for my life and thoughts of hope and opportunity for my two young grandchildren.

I hope that someday they will find this memoir amusing and informative about the way things were for their grandparents in another place and time. May they meet the challenges, avoid the misfortunes, and enjoy the blessings of their own times, and live long, happy and productive lives.

Anna and Nathan Gockley. (Photo by Beatrice Gockley)

ADDENDUM

Following is a tongue-in-cheek piece I wrote and delivered at the Doughty family reunion following Uncle Bud's death in 2001. It was intended as amusement for the large gathering of relatives and as a quirky tribute to Bud—the kind he would have liked.

Uncle Bud's Second Will

I, Charles M. Buddy Doughty, being of half decent mind and, oh, purty good body, add these things to my last will and testament.

My brother Wendell can take care of the other one. And you'll probbly have to clean out my apartment too, Wendell. Don't throw out any matchbook covers. They might be worth something. See if you can get Bruce to help, and maybe Voni (Clark) Doody.

You all know I never had nothin' but I'd like to leave a couple little things to a few people. Maybe they'll remember me, you know.

First, to my niece Voni. She's been trying to clean me up these last few years. I want her to have the only new thing I own, never been out of its wrapper. It's Ivory soap, of course!

And to her sister Glenda Spittle, I'd like to leave the name I gave her when she was little, the wee Diddidarro.

To Billy Hansen, who always wanted Madeline's attention the same time I did, until he growed up, I leave an old mouth organ I found on the C & P tracks behind the Smoke Shop in 1954. I hear he likes them blues.

To my far-away nephew and big deal mirror polisher, David Hilyard, I'd like to leave a very special trick that a lot of you have seen and maybe even tried. But I hear that David has a lot of my Doughty humor and music in him, and this will go good at them California wine and hot-tub parties, as long as people keep their shirt on. What you do, Dave, is go up to somebody in the middle of something important, grab their shirtsleeve between your thumb and finger, shake it good and hard, then snap it—"Awwbverreech!

His brother, Junior, has been going to school so long he's overqualified for just about everything, except being a shrink. But I'm going to leave him some advice on what to do when he gets really fed up with the boss. Raise hell and shit in the brook! You can do that in Alaska.

To my niece Cheryl (Estey) Gilmore, who also has

my kind of humor—even worse—I want to leave one of my favorite songs (I hear she still remembers how it goes): "Hi-dee-hey and a hi-dee-ho, listen to the radio, pahdaw pahdaw, pahdaw pahdaw."

Teddy Smith, he likes a good laugh and he likes to build stuff, like his father. So I want him to have my squeegee for a mograb. It's been used a lot but it's still good.

To my nephew Hal, who's spent too much time in the woods, I want to leave what I learned about getting along with a woman: "She is but she ain't, she ain't but she is."

To my nephew Carl (he already inherited my Doughty temper), I'll leave my secret for staying cool, calm, and collected when you skin your knuckles, stub your toe, or bang your head. Holler at the top of your lungs, "Skiddaballs! Hoppose!"

To my nurse nieces, like Jane (Doughty) Prior, Pam (Doughty) Harpine, Judy Hilyard, and Wanda (Hilyard) Gonzales, and maybe a thousand others by now, I'll leave my remedy for what to do when your patients come down with the hypopoppalis: LEMONADE (that's beer). Doesn't matter what kind. Beer's beer. It's good for what ails you.

To my nephew Don Doughty, who's always been a good worker, I'll leave my doodiddidaw. It's like new. I never figured out what it's good for. Maybe he can.

To my nephew Ronnie Doughty, who's always been a good boy and a little on the quiet side, I want to leave my foolish noises. They come in handy when things get too quiet, or too serious.

To my niece Marjorie (everyone knows her by her quick laugh), I'll leave my moodiness, just for a change of pace. That way people will wonder what's wrong or what they said. She can have some fun with that.

To them good-looking daughters of my brother Clarence, Alice, Betty, Dorothy, Verlie, and Sandra, I'll leave a picture of me in my military police uniform. They can fight over it or make as many copies as they want. Why should I pay for them? Can't afford it.

To the family of my brother Bruce, who is almost as foolish as I am and a role model for my own dreams of police work, I leave my billy club and handcuffs. They can be handed down to each generation along with all Bruce's stuff.

To my niece Joyce (Doughty) McDougall, I leave my secret map of how to cross the border into Canada without anybody knowing. Notice that Maine is a lot bigger than Canada—but not as big as Massachusetts.

To any niece or grandniece who's getting too fat, I'll leave my secret to being just skin and bones—and my ten-year supply of sardines. (Didn't know I had that, did you? Some people might be educated but they don't know everything.) Just have one can a day, a cup of coffee, maybe a banana. Before long, I guarantee you'll look just like me. It helps if you tramp the streets.

To all my other nieces and nephews, hey, I only got so much foolishness. I tried to pass on as much as I could when you were growing up. Some took and some didn't. I hope you all remember a little bit of it, so you won't forget your old Uncle Bud.

To my grandnephew Shawn Cote, who is a purty good artist and writer, I leave my picture of a Seebeelump dreamed up by my brother Harry. Maybe it'll inspire him.

I'd like to save another grandnephew, Heath Hilyard, from going off the deep end in Republican politics. So I'm leaving him all my old newspaper clippings of the Kennedy family. He might learn something. I know I give way too much to the Hilyards already, but this boy needs all the help he can get. It might be important to the whole world someday.

To any grandnephew who's planning to go somewhere and is not over five-foot-six and no more than a hunderd pounds soakin' wet, I'll leave my one good suit I got off of Sawyer George in 1955—very best quality—unless you want to bury me in it. Then, too bad.

To my other grandnieces and nephews, you probbly already have too much stuff. If not, you can have anything you want from the stuff Wendell and Bruce throw out of my apartment before they take it to the dump.

Finally, I'd like to leave something really special to Bubby Fields, but I can't think of anything else. I hear he has more than enough of my best traits already. They say he's the one that's the most like me.

Except for David Estey. He's the one that used to pal around with me the most. He's always been smart like me, and with good humor. So I'm leavin' him all the rest of my foolishness. He can add it to what he learned workin' for the guvmint.

To my brothers and sisters who are left, I tried to save what shekels I could for you by eating sardines all those years. Actually, I always hated sardines, so I hope you appreciate it.

To the town of Fort Fairfield, where I was born, growed up, and lived all my life—where they let me tramp the streets, give me jobs, and kind of looked out for me—I leave my free spirit, love of nonsense, patriotism, and town pride. I know I'm not the only character in town, but when they made me, they broke the mold.

Well, that's it, then. As they say in the movies, "Adios, amigos." Don't take any wooden nickels.

David Estey for Charles M. Doughty

ACKNOWLEDGMENTS

First of all, I want to thank Carl Little and Kathryn Olmstead for their generous and perceptive endorsements. I also want to thank the entire crew at Maine Authors Publishing & Cooperative in Rockland, especially Jane Ekland, for her excellent editing, and David Allen, for designing and managing production of the artistic book I envisioned. I was inspired to do the memoir after reading *Happy Days Along the Kennebec* by William Webb and *It's Time To Tell Our Stories, 1858-2008*, a history of Fort Fairfield, by Rayle Reed Ainsworth and Sarah Ulman. I was encouraged by my good friends Joanne Boynton and Jane Phillips to write down the stories I have loved to tell over the years. Finally, I want to thank my wife, Karen, for her love and enthusiastic support for all of my endeavors.

ABOUT THE AUTHOR

DAVID ESTEY was born in Fort Fairfield and raised in the heart of Aroostook County, Maine. He is now a fine-arts painter in coastal Belfast and a retired IRS regional public affairs manager for five mid-Atlantic States and Washington, D.C.

Besides raising a family and completing a 31-year federal career, he has lived, taught, exhibited and sold his art in Baltimore/Washington, Philadelphia, PA, Charlotte, NC and mid-coast Maine. His work is in 18 states and seven countries.

He has a BFA degree in painting from Rhode Island School of Design and an MSA degree in public administration from George Washington University. He studied art for a year in Rome, Italy, 14 years at Pennsylvania Academy of the Fine Arts, and several sessions at Haystack Mountain School of Crafts.

He and his wife, Karen, live in their home and studio overlooking Belfast Harbor. For more information, visit his website at **www.davidestey.com**.